Four-Mallet Marimba Playing

A Musical Approach for All Levels

by Nancy Zeltsman

Edited by Rick Mattingly

Photos by Andy Ryan

ISBN 0-634-03426-X

7777 W. Bluemound Rd. P.O. Box 13819 Milwaukee, WI 53213

Visit Hal Leonard Online at
www.halleonard.com

Table of Contents

(A) = requires a 4-1/3-octave (low-A) marimba
(F) = requires a 4-1/2-octave (low-F) marimba
(E) = requires a 4-1/2-octave (low-E) marimba
(A/5), (A/E), (F/5) = can be played on different-sized marimbas noted, depending on register
All other pieces in **Section IV** and **Section V** require a 5-octave (low-C) marimba.

To my parents,
Martha and Joe Zeltsman

Pedagogical Approaches

Many people view committing to serious, specialized study of the marimba as extremely risky. That attitude explains why many colleges, universities, and conservatories are reluctant or opposed to recognizing marimba as a separate area of study from percussion. Administrators and teachers cite the fact that extremely few people in the world enjoy any kind of real success as marimbists—which is true, if you measure success only in financial rewards and professional demand.

First, I believe that people should be able to study what they are passionate about. Second, I think there are viable ways to forge a career as a marimbist, if one is creative about it, and that—relative to the grossly excessive number of people being trained to be well-rounded percussionists (under the pretense that *that* is a practical venture)—it is in fact quite a reasonable pursuit. Third, no one chooses a career in music for its financial rewards, so it's silly to hold them up as a measuring stick.

Success comes in many forms. Those of us who specialize on marimba have known the satisfaction and, often, the thrill of being a pioneer in a new field. To be a marimbist, you must thrive on challenge. I was seduced first by the instrument itself but, ultimately, with all that comes with it: the uphill battle to familiarize people with it, creating opportunities for oneself, finding/generating repertoire, and even elevating the artistry of playing it. When every aspect of your field is a challenge, small successes can seem larger and be quite meaningful. In the big picture, there is the gratification that your efforts have the chance to make an impact in the evolution of the instrument.

I am among the first generation of those who teach marimba as a specialty and whose teachers were, by and large, *not* marimbists but percussionists or other instrumentalists. This book basically lays out what is, to date, "my school" of marimba playing. What I have arrived at (so far) and present in this book reflects the wisdom of my teachers (or at least what I was able to take from them) funneled through my personal tastes and interests and what I learned in the course of following my own career path.

My colleagues have developed their own schools of playing through a similar process, yet our resulting approaches and philosophies in some cases differ significantly. Nevertheless, we have each dedicated most of our lives to this pursuit and, naturally, feel strongly about the opinions we have formed.

I've encountered quite a few students who are perplexed by the differing approaches of different players/teachers. When students have been working hard to absorb knowledge from one teacher and then meet another specialist who doesn't agree with something they're doing, it can be very disheartening. A student can suddenly feel in a quandary, or even panicked, about which way is "right." This doesn't happen only in relation to the marimba; reconciling different teachers' approaches is part of learning in general. But, in the case of marimba, it's important for students to be aware of the context in which teachers may differ.

Concert marimba performance and pedagogy is a very young field. My colleagues and I are doing our best to present to students concepts we believe with all our hearts. But we are all still just "trying them on for size." Most of us have only been at this for a few decades. By comparison, consider that the performance practices of the violin, cello, and piano are centuries old. Famous pedagogues on those instruments studied with famous pedagogues, who studied with famous pedagogues. To study with any one of those teachers, you would stand to gain their personal perspectives as well as a sense of history.

I was a very serious student when I was young. While I studied with each of my primary teachers, I took their opinions as "gospel"—as *the* way things should be done. I tried to follow their lead in every aspect of my playing.

Trying to soak up everything you can from someone you trust can be an extremely beneficial way to learn. There's a purity to it, and it can keep you extremely focused. Sometimes it requires accepting certain premises on faith before they entirely make sense to you but, oftentimes, they *will* make sense once you can see the larger picture the teacher is laying out. Some of the most profound truths only become clear once you are entirely immersed in someone's approach to their craft: that larger Gestalt. If, in time, you understand not only how a teacher would recommend you do something, but how that teacher *arrives* at how things should be done—that is, how that person *thinks*—you will have learned the richest lesson. From studying like this, I learned to think for myself.

People have different capacities to be able to think for themselves—that is, to be able to identify questions or problems, seek out information or solutions, and to integrate that knowledge into their existing worldview. Usually, the ones who can are the most successful.

There are certainly other ways to study. You might study seriously with different people for short periods, or take a few lessons with many different people. Studying with more than one specialist can lead to a broader view and be very helpful. However, it requires that you are very good at thinking for yourself. You must be able to sift through a lot of information and opinions and be able to make sound judgments about which ones "ring true" to you; which ones will make sense within *your* evolving Gestalt.

Whether you choose to immerse yourself in the principles of one marimba teacher for a period of a few years, or seize opportunities to study occasionally with many different marimba teachers, in the end, I suggest you take it all "with a grain of salt." I don't mean that you shouldn't dearly cherish or trust what you've been taught. I just think that the newness of marimba performance practices means that marimba students need to: (1) accept that more contradictions and discrepancies may exist between schools of playing than is the case with most other instruments; (2) understand that this is "part of the territory"; and (3) accept more responsibility than most other instrumentalists in deciding which concepts hold merit.

This is also why it is an exciting time to be a marimbist. Anyone playing the marimba today who does excellent, creative work stands to make a vital contribution to the marimba's advancement. It is incumbent on the next generations of marimba players to combine ideas from various schools of playing, to let your imagination run wild with possibility, to experiment, and to gradually, through time, weave together the points that make the most sense (that is, reap the most musical results) into a richer marimba performance practice.

There are many ways to learn. Sometimes something one teacher or friend says doesn't sink in, while another person may be able to frame the same concept in a way that reaches you personally. This is why it is important to hear as many players as possible and expose yourself to as many schools of thought as possible. Broaden your base by attending all kinds of concerts, having contact with teachers of other instruments, listening to recordings, and discussing all of this with friends. Where and when the most eye-opening revelations occur may surprise you.

This book lays out one approach. You will undoubtedly come upon differences of opinion between your various teachers, or between your teacher(s) and opinions I express in this book. Don't be discouraged or frustrated by this. Try not to discount any advice you receive or any information you are exposed to. Instead, realize that the contradictions and discrepancies are part of the thrilling stage we are at in the marimba's history.

Hopefully, many of the ideas contained here will be of interest to you, or worth considering—or perhaps they will lead you, in combination with advice from your teachers or colleagues, to make some discoveries. Your ultimate goal should be to realize a way of playing that feels right to you.

Acknowledgments

My deepest thanks to Steve Mackey, who cheerfully endured my frequent preoccupation with this book during the many months it took to write and the years it was in planning. He was a constant source of support and encouragement and provided invaluable suggestions as the manuscript's first reader. Also, very special thanks to the book's next six readers who provided astute feedback in the final stage before I submitted the manuscript: Gary Cook, Ray Dillard, Jack Van Geem, Samuel Z. Solomon, Fumito Nunoya, and Seth Woodard. Warmest thanks to all the students with whom I have worked (especially my masters marimba students at The Boston Conservatory) who have so deeply enriched my life and taught me incredible lessons about the marimba, performing, and people. I could not have written this without you. Much love and thanks to my parents for driving me to hundreds of music lessons, and for your incredible support of my somewhat eccentric career path.

I am so grateful to Rick Mattingly, who first asked me to consider writing this book, advised me along the way, and who is such a fine, thoughtful editor. Thanks to the great team at Hal Leonard who assembled the book. Thanks to Andy Ryan for his fantastic photographs. Finally, thanks to Berklee College of Music (for a Berklee Faculty Development Grant, which assisted in the early stages of writing this book), Nancy Ubick (at Hal Leonard), Paula Matthews (at Princeton University's Mendel Music Library), and Linda Golding.

Setting out to write a marimba method book, I found I couldn't help wanting to model it, to some degree, on Morris Goldenberg's *Modern School for Xylophone, Marimba, Vibraphone*, which has been a cornerstone in mallet percussion pedagogy for over fifty years. Unlike Goldenberg, I have included considerable instructional material, but still, many of the pages are filled with music. It is impossible to really grow as a musician without playing a lot of music, and I hope the music included here will be a useful addition to the repertoire.

The marimba, which arrived at its modern incarnation in the early 1900s, is now, a century later, well on its way to being recognized as a dignified concert instrument that can stand on its own apart from the family of percussion instruments. It is also beginning to leave behind its reputation as a Vaudeville/novelty instrument.

This book centers around four-mallet technique, the predominant approach to marimba playing today, as opposed to two-mallet technique, which was the focus of Goldenberg's book. Although I seriously studied two-mallet technique for several years—mostly applied to the xylophone, and under the supervision of a phenomenal two-mallet player, Ian Finkel—today it is extremely rare that I play marimba with two mallets. Personally, I prefer the feel of holding four mallets. I would hold four mallets even if I were playing something quite simple. With an easy piece, utilizing four mallets can facilitate my having to move around less and, therefore, allow me to feel more at ease and more able to focus on musical issues (see Section I-E: Basics of Four-Mallet Stickings).

From Ian Finkel (with whom I studied all the mallet instruments—xylophone, marimba, vibraphone—in my late high school years), I developed the sense that the combination of the xylophone, two-mallet playing, and fast lines was a "natural," and that the combination of the marimba, four-mallet playing, and slightly slower, thicker textures was a natural. It makes sense; the narrower width of xylophone bars (in most cases) means they can be traversed more rapidly. Since the lower half of the marimba is far more resonant than the xylophone, slower lines are more idiomatic on that instrument; they give the resonance a chance to blossom. The music that best flatters the xylophone versus the marimba might be compared with music suited to the violin versus the cello. Of course, the polyphonic potential of four-mallet playing is a significant factor in the elevation of the marimba's stature as a solo instrument.

Ian Finkel also taught me "traditional" four-mallet grip. I don't remember the specifics of how Ian explained it, so I will describe it as it has worked for me. It's the only grip I have ever used because it has always felt comfortable and suited me well. While it is widely used in Asia and parts of Europe, in the last decade or so it has become less commonly used in the United States. I hope this text will clarify the strengths of traditional grip relative to other grips and encourage its use (see Section I–B: Traditional Four-Mallet Grip).

However, if another grip already works well for you, I see no reason for you to switch to traditional grip. People's hands are different, and it is perfectly plausible that you might prefer another grip. In that case, I hope you will still make use of this book and consider applying some of the other concepts I introduce to your own style of playing.

My goal is that this book will help to fill a number of voids I have discovered in the course of teaching marimba. As I write this, there is a tremendous shortage of good four-mallet marimba music for beginning and intermediate players who need practice coordinating different configurations of notes, and who are eager to understand some of the basic technical moves of marimba playing. To help meet these needs, I have composed 50 Short Four-Mallet Studies (Section II).

There is also a limited quantity of high-quality music suited to the intermediate student. In Section IV: 18 Intermediate-to-Advanced Adapted Solos, I offer some additions to the existing literature. Most of these pieces are appropriate for recitals, auditions, or juries.

I discovered many of these solos through searches in music libraries. I encourage players who enjoy these pieces to make their own treks to libraries. Begin by looking through music for piano, guitar, harp, violin, and cello. Give special consideration to music and composers off the beaten path; these can often lead to adaptations of great value and character. Just *looking* will expand and deepen your knowledge of music. The scores you bring home for further consideration will be a means to improve your sight-reading skills. Let your imagination run wild as you explore the possibilities of what could work effectively on the marimba. You will also find that this is a fabulous means toward developing a personal repertoire. I will say more on this in Section III–F: Building a Personal Repertoire.

The book is laid out in such a way as to suggest a general progression of study, but it's fine to skip around, too. In general, Section II is mostly playable if you understand all the basics from Section I, but some information in Section III will be helpful when playing some pieces in Section II. In general, there is information in both Section I and III that could provide some good review material, or at least food for thought, to people at many different stages in their development.

Throughout the book, stickings are numbered left to right, with 1 being the bass mallet and 4 being the soprano mallet.

It may go without saying but, although I have provided guidelines about basic good musicianship, I do recommend that students study much of the music in this book with a teacher. I know that I learned a lot by playing through the studies in Goldenberg's book, but with the guidance of a teacher they came alive in ways I wouldn't have otherwise seen. Oftentimes, you don't necessarily need a percussion teacher, per se, to give you helpful musical feedback. In my formative years I received brilliant coaching on phrasing from my high school band director, Donald Marrs, whose main instrument was euphonium.

This book is for players of all levels:

Beginners. This book is targeted to beginners of marimba study who already have a basic knowledge of reading rhythms and music written in both treble and bass clef. Some candidates are: (a) high school-level drumset players and/or percussionists who want to begin serious study of four-mallet marimba playing or who need extra work on marimba to prepare for their college audition; (b) college-level drumset players and/or percussionists who need more mallet experience; or (c) adult beginners.

Intermediate players. Examples: (a) people who haven't been playing marimba long but came to it with a strong background in piano; or (b) high school or college-level players with a solid foundation in mallet playing who seek good repertoire from which to gain more experience.

Advanced players. There are an enormous number of players who have come to learn difficult repertoire completely by memory. They desperately need a collection of material for working on their four-mallet sight-reading.

Players interested in studying examples of important repertoire for marimba will be interested in Section V: Advanced Solos and Chamber Music. My inspiration for this was the section of orchestral excerpts that Goldenberg included at the end of his book. Here, I discuss three recommended marimba solos and three chamber works for violin and marimba (and, in two cases, an additional player or tape) drawn from the library of nearly eighty pieces that I premiered with violinist Sharan Leventhal as the duo Marimolin during 1985–1996. With the exception of Andrew Thomas' "Merlin," the pieces in Section V were all dedicated to/composed for me. My commentary is based on experiences learning these pieces and coaching from the composers. Each composer has endorsed my comments.

Many of the pieces in this book require a five-octave marimba. I strongly support five octaves becoming the standardized range of marimbas and, thankfully, many institutions have already acquired a five-octave instrument. However, all of the studies in Section II can be played on a four-and-one-third-octave (low A) marimba. The size of the marimba required for all the pieces in Section IV and V can be seen at a glance in the Table of Contents (the key is at the end).

In summary, this book is intended for every marimbist. In particular, I hope it holds meaning for those players whose passion for musical expression overshadows concerns with technique. The future of the instrument is in your capable hands.

Nancy Zeltsman
Boston, Massachusetts (2003)

Choosing Mallets

The quality of sound you produce on marimba is determined by the mallets you select, the quality of the instrument, and the particular way you strike the bar, also known as your "touch." Most serious players have accumulated and rely upon a wide variety of mallets. Factors contributing to which mallets are used for a certain piece include the character of the music, the register(s) of the marimba to be played, the specific marimba, and the acoustics of the room. It is not uncommon for players to change mallets in the middle of a piece, if time permits, when shifts of character or register occur. In general, softer mallets are most flattering to lower notes and harder mallets are most flattering to higher notes.

An array of mallets could be compared to an oil painter's palette. Just as darker, muted shades of paint are often selected to express a rich, warm atmosphere, softer mallets achieve a darker, warmer tone (by emphasizing the fundamental tone and suppressing the bright harmonics). Brighter paints might be compared to harder mallets, which produce sharper-edged tones (by emphasizing brighter harmonics and supplying a clear point of attack).

There are an enormous number of commercially marketed mallets available. What differentiates them is the hardness (or softness) of the mallet and the characteristics of the tone they produce. The determining factors are the shape of the mallet head, the material(s) from which the head is made, the weight of the head, the type of outer covering (which is usually yarn), the type of yarn used, how tightly the yarn is wrapped, and the type of handle.

Some players make their own mallets. It isn't difficult but can be time-consuming. Some players buy commercial mallets but occasionally re-wrap the yarn heads themselves. (Different colored yarns are frequently used to enable players to quickly distinguish between their mallets.)

Mallet handles are made of fiberglass, plastic, rattan, or wood (birch or maple). Almost all professionals use rattan or wood. Rattan handles are somewhat flexible, which some find is easier on their hands than wood. Rattan comes from a plant that grows with joints, like bamboo. (Its long, slender, tough stems

are also used in wickerwork.) There is a limit to the length of a rattan shoot that is straight, of an even diameter, and free of knots. Wooden handles, therefore, appeal to many marimbists because they can be a bit longer, which accommodates wide intervals. Personally, I find wood more comfortable; the stiffness of the handles gives me the feeling I can direct the mallet heads with greater precision.

A beginning marimbist will be fine with just one good set of four mallets. A basic, all-purpose set should have a pleasant, warm sound without a hard attack (which could become grating on your ears). The main thing I would caution against is "hard," or even many "medium-hard," mallets. Start with "medium" or, depending on the manufacturer, even "medium-soft."

In my opinion, many mallets are labeled on the hard side. This may be because they are geared toward drum corps or marching band playing in which projection and "cutting through" is essential. But here we're concerned with solo marimba playing, so a slightly mellower attack is more appropriate.

I believe that mallets with a horizontal-oval-shape head (like Encore Mallets' Nancy Zeltsman Series) have the potential to produce the fullest tone. Perhaps this is because marimba bars are made of vertical-grain wood. Therefore, a wide mallet head would set the most vertical grains vibrating. Also, mallets with slightly heavy heads tend to produce a fuller sound than lighter-weight ones. Of the mallets I helped develop made by Encore, I would recommend that beginners first purchase either: (1) two pairs of NZ3s (green); (2) one pair NZ3s and one pair of NZ4s (mocha); or (3) the NZ Graduated Set of 4. See Section III–E: Refining Mallet Selection.

1B Traditional Four-Mallet Grip

In this chapter, I will refer to fingers following the method used by pianists: 1st (or thumb), 2nd, 3rd, 4th and 5th.

There are two general approaches to holding two mallets in each hand.

1. Cross grips: This category includes "traditional" grip and Burton grip. In each of these, the mallet handles are crossed. With traditional grip, each pair of mallets is held in an X configuration, usually with the outer mallet of each hand underneath the inner mallet (although sometimes this is reversed). With Burton grip, the inner mallet of each hand is underneath the outer mallet, and each pair of mallets is held in more of a + configuration. In both grips, the hands are generally positioned slightly "choked up" from the ends of the mallet handles.
2. Independent-mallet grips: This category includes Musser grip and Stevens grip. With these, one mallet is held by the 4th and 5th fingers; the other is held with the 1st, 2nd, and 3rd fingers. The mallets' handles are held near the ends. In general, these grips require quite a bit of small-muscle strength and, therefore, can be more difficult to develop.

Most players select one of these grips and use it all the time. A minority of players feel comfortable with more than one grip and choose a particular grip for a particular situation. There are even a few players who use a different grip in each hand. There are fabulous players who use each of the main grips as well as variations on them. So, clearly, no grip is better than all of the others; they each have their advantages. Also, there are many different types of hands. Most people can learn traditional grip easily, but some can't. Those who find it difficult often have short fingers, or weak 4th and 5th fingers.

Traditional four-mallet grip has been extremely comfortable for me and best suits my musical priorities and style of playing. I will elaborate on its advantages at the end of this chapter.

12 STEPS TO LEARNING TRADITIONAL GRIP

Throughout these steps, I will be referring to the four mallets with the following number system:

Mallet:	1	2	3	4
	(outer)	(inner)	(inner)	(outer)
	left hand		right hand	

STEP 1: "Back" fingers

Lay out the four mallets in two pairs with the handles crossed. The outer mallet handles should be on the bottom: that is, mallets 1 and 4. It helps to have the handles extending off the marimba (or a table). See Photo 1.

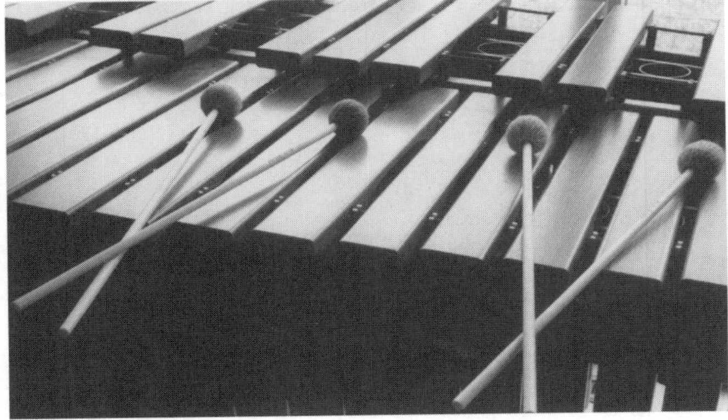

photo 1

I suggest starting with your dominant hand. Put your 2nd finger down through the top of the X (where the mallets cross). See Photo 2.

photo 2

Wrap your 4th and 5th fingers around the crossed handles keeping the mallets stacked, with the outer handle on the bottom. The 4th and 5th fingers must stretch across the mallets, curl and touch the palm of your hand. See Photo 3

photo 3

The 5th finger (and sometimes the 4th, too) will always touch your palm and sometimes needs to hold the mallet shafts very firmly.

If you have long fingers, it may help to think of your 4th and 5th fingers as extending flat across the mallets to the heel of your hand, as opposed to being curled around the mallets. This will avoid the fingernails of your 4th and 5th fingers digging uncomfortably into your palm.

The 4th finger will often help the 5th finger anchor the mallets. Other times, it will be relaxed and loosely curled around the sticks (not reaching over to the palm). See if you can clench your 4th and 5th fingers—the same way you clench to make a fist. Now try to do it with just your 5th finger. Can you clench your 5th finger and wiggle your 4th finger? For some people, those fingers prefer to work in tandem. If this is true for you, hold down your 5th finger (using your other hand), and try to wiggle your 4th finger. You may need to practice isolating the movements of these two fingers.

STEP 2: "Front" fingers, focus on 2nd finger

Your 1st and 2nd fingers will *always* be between the two mallets. The outer stick will contact the fleshy spot on the side of your 2nd finger, midway between the first two joints. Think of this spot as "home base" for the outer stick. It helps to bend your 2nd finger slightly in order to see the definition of your joints. See Photo 4.

You can also orient the outer stick to your 2nd finger just above the first joint, either all the time, or occasionally, if that is more comfortable. But since a blister in that spot runs the risk of infecting your fingernail, I recommend beginning with the lower orientation point between the first two joints.

The 3rd finger gently cradles the outer mallet. You should keep the 3rd finger loosely curled at all times. If it becomes tightly curled around the outer stick, it will prevent you from being able to bring the two mallets together to play small intervals.

photo 4

STEP 3: "Front" fingers/focus on thumb

The thumb should rest on top of the inside mallet. It is important to bend the thumb slightly in order to see the definition of the joints. There are two main orientation points on the outside of the thumb for the inner mallet: (1) just above the first joint: that is, between the thumbnail and the first joint (see Photo 5); (2) just below the first joint (see Photo 6).

photo 5

photo 6

With the thumb bent slightly, the mallet handle can find a little groove to push into—and feel anchored—in these spots. The spot above the first joint tends to be most comfortable for intervals of a fourth or smaller. The spot below the first joint tends to be most comfortable for intervals of a fifth or larger. The optimum placement of the thumb on the inside mallet will vary depending on the register in which you're playing.

One warning for people with double-jointed thumbs (ones that can curl outward into a hook shape): You must resist curling your thumb like this; rather, bend the tip of the thumb inward, enough to reveal the definition of the joints. When the double-jointed curl occurs, the smoothness of the outside of the thumb makes it much more difficult to find one of those grooves in which you can anchor the stick.

There are some other possible orientation points along the side of the thumb. Notice that, if you move the stick from below the first joint very slightly further down the thumb, the mallet handle can find another groove before the second joint, as shown in Photo 7.

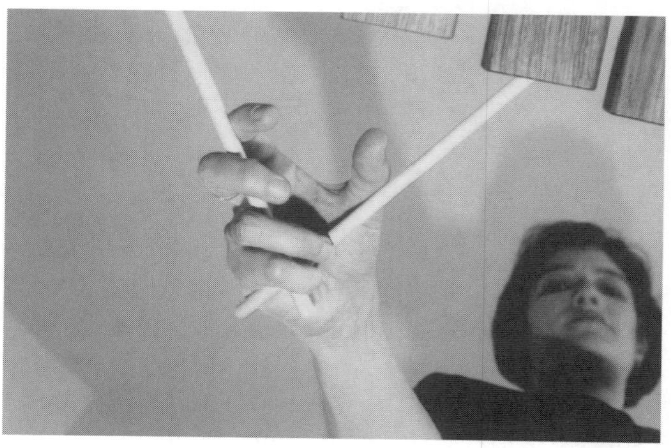

photo 7

There is another groove below the second joint. As the mallet goes lower and lower on the thumb, you will notice that, in the "back" (palm) of your hand, it becomes difficult to keep your 4th finger across both mallets. As the inside mallet's orientation point becomes lower on the thumb, you will need to hold the mallets in the back with only the 5th finger.

You have probably noticed that gradually lowering the inside mallet's orientation point to the thumb results in a gradually wider space between the two mallets of that hand. This enables you to play wider and wider intervals. It is unnecessary to concern yourself too much at this time with intervals beyond an octave. But to get an idea of what is possible, you can extend the orientation point of the inner mallet way down into the fleshy part of your palm. You'll find that the inner mallet will then be "held" in the back simply by its resting on the inner side of the tip of the 5th finger, and the fact that the end of that mallet is wedged into the fleshy part of the outside of your hand.

OVERVIEW 1

By clenching the 5th finger (and maybe also 4th finger) around the X, they are essentially pushing *up* and providing resistance, against which the 1st and 2nd fingers can push *down*. That pressure you apply with the 1st and 2nd fingers can make the mallets feel really anchored—almost "glued"—to those fingers. If you play a lot, you will probably form a blister, and then callus, on the 2nd finger at the orientation point, and possibly also on the primary orientation points on your thumb.

So far, I have stressed the notions of "clenching" and "pressure" in order to explain the basic premise of traditional grip. But as you become more comfortable with it, you will discover ways to minimize the physical tensions involved and the muscles in your hand will develop. You will eventually come to feel that the 4th and 5th fingers can provide solid support of the mallets with ease.

STEP 4: Basic double-stops, body posture, low mallet-positioning

Play a comfortable-sized interval with both mallets (that is, a double-stop); try an interval of a fourth, fifth, or sixth. Repeat it slowly, playing quarter notes at a metronome mark of about quarter note = 70. Try to play with a full sound, at a dynamic of ***mf*** to ***mp***.

As you do so, think about your basic body posture. You should have both feet on the floor with your weight distributed evenly between them and be standing up straight, squarely facing the marimba. You want your arms to feel very relaxed and long, extending from your shoulders, with elbows in and relaxed.

Your palms should be facing down, rather than having your hands rotated with the thumbs up. Your basic strokes, up and down from the wrists, will be similar to that of matched-grip snare drum playing. See Photo 8.

photo 8

To practice good, relaxed arm extension, try some strokes in which you allow the mallet handles to touch the bars (it won't harm them). Then try some strokes in which, just after you play, your mallet heads come to a resting point just above the keyboard. I'll expand on this idea in Section I–D: Basic Strokes and Tone Production.

In general, I advocate keeping your mallets fairly low to the keyboard as you play. There are four reasons for this:

1. Your movements across the keyboard will look very smooth.
2. You'll feel most connected to the keyboard (it's the closest we can come to emulating a pianist's hands actually being in contact with the keyboard).
3. You'll take advantage of the greatest surface area of the mallet striking the bar, for the "fattest" sound.
4. You'll have the best chance at note accuracy.

STEP 5: One-time exercise revealing power potential

You can still play with plenty of power with your mallets relatively low by taking advantage of the power in your wrists. To get a feel for the power reserves available in your wrists, I suggest doing a somewhat strange exercise just a few times. It involves an awkward movement that I would *not* suggest you continue to practice, but it is a concise way to feel the muscles available to you.

First, from about a foot over the marimba, play a rather heavy double-stop downstroke, using the weight of your arm. Afterward, "freeze" with the mallet heads just above the keyboard; your wrist will also be low to the keyboard. Now, keeping your wrist low, lift the mallets up very slowly, bending up from your wrist to an exaggerated degree, as shown in photo 9.

photo 9

When you can't strain your wrist any more, allow the mallets to snap down heavily again. Repeat this heavy, fast downstroke and exaggerated, slow upstroke several times at about *mf*. Imagine you are playing on beat one of a 5/4 bar at quarter note = 70, taking the next four slow beats to raise the mallets.

What this should demonstrate is that your wrists' resistance (while in a low position) against raising your mallets makes available tremendous power when the wrist snaps down. You can also play with a similar amount of power keeping your mallets generally much lower, using a modest amount of wrist snap.

STEP 6: Catching up the other hand

Put your opposite hand through steps 1 through 5. Try to do everything absolutely symmetrically to the first hand, matching the clean, natural movements of your stronger hand and wrist.

OVERVIEW 2

Whenever the mallets feel like they're slipping, or you feel you're losing the basic orientation points for the 2nd finger and thumb, or the mallet handles are clicking together, the problem will probably be that you don't have a firm enough grip with the 5th finger around the mallets at the back of your hand.

STEP 7: Medium-to-large intervals

So far, I have described the basic grip for conservatively-sized intervals (fourths through sixths). Here are more details about shifting between medium-to-large-sized intervals.

Starting with your dominant hand, play a fourth—for example, a C and F—a few times. By stretching out with the 2nd finger, open the F out to a G and play the fifth (C and G) a few times. In opening to the fifth, the thumb may also want to stretch out slightly in the opposite direction and the thumb orientation point *may* go from the spot above the first joint to below the first joint (or it may not, depending on your hand).

Next, open out to a sixth (C and A) and play that double-stop a few times. With the sixth, the thumb orientation point *is* likely to be most comfortable below the first joint. (If you have small hands, you may find it easier if the orientation point on the 2nd finger shifts up above the first joint. Review STEP 2. But if you're comfortable with the 2nd finger orientation point remaining between the first two joints, that is preferable.)

Keep opening out to a seventh, then an octave, and then (if you're daring) a ninth or tenth, depending on the width of your bars and the register you're in. With intervals of a seventh or wider, you may need to hold onto the X with only your 5th finger. Your 4th finger should then be loosely curled and relaxed, even though the 5th finger is still clenching. With wide intervals, you can use the tip of the 4th finger to press on the outer mallet to anchor it. See Photo 7. (This is one way to "lock" your interval size.) Also, the thumb orientation point may change to farther back on your thumb to the little groove just above the second joint (see Photo 10) or even below it. (Review the last paragraph of STEP 3.) Play each double-stop a few times.

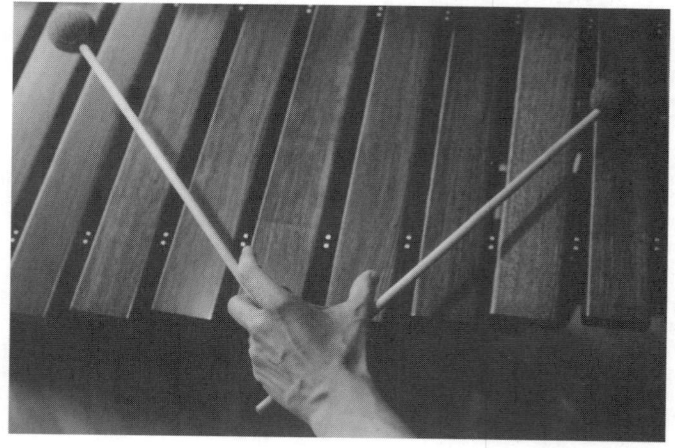

photo 10

Now work your way closed: octave, seventh, sixth, fifth, fourth—noting slight adjustments along the way. For example, by the time you are as small as a sixth or fifth, your 4th finger may be able to come back across the X, rejoining the 5th finger in clenching mode. The thumb orientation points may change along the way. Basically, to state the obvious, you're gradually bringing your fist closed. For an interval of a third (C to E), the most comfortable thumb orientation point will almost definitely be the spot above the first joint.

I urge you to invent some exercises in which you concentrate on various patterns of interval shifts. This could include keeping the inner mallet on the same note and gradually widening and narrowing the intervals, as described above. Or, keep the outer mallet on the same note and gradually expand and contract the interval size with the inner mallet. Or, shift repeatedly between intervals such as a fourth and sixth, or third and fifth, or fifth and octave.

STEP 8: Small intervals

One slightly tricky thing is the interval of a second. For this interval, you need to get your 2nd finger forward and out of the way. Straighten it out, but be careful to keep the tip of it hooked under the outside mallet. The tip of your thumb should be hooked under the inside mallet.

Your thumb will help to bring the mallets closed for this small interval by pushing down on the inside mallet and, using a sort of downward "scooping" pressure, pulling it in toward the 2nd finger. Remember: you can push down with the thumb against the resistance offered by the 4th and 5th fingers clenching upward. See Photo 11.

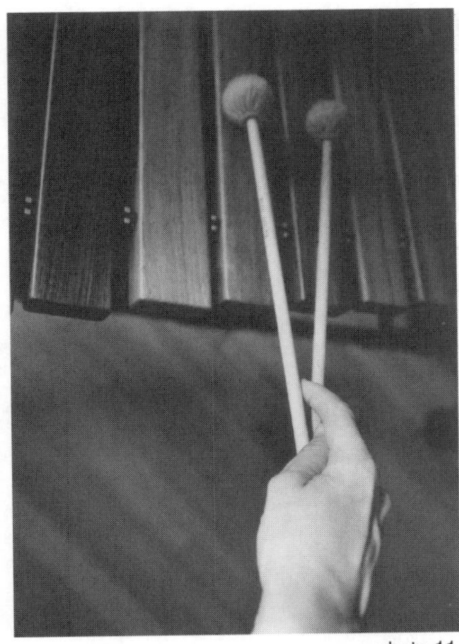

photo 11

It is crucial that you keep both the thumb and 2nd finger in between the two mallets; otherwise, you won't be able to open back out to regular position. With the interval of a second, your 3rd finger will be wrapped around both mallets underneath along with the 4th and 5th fingers.

When you go from the interval of a second back to a third, you're reclaiming the basic position; with the interval of a third, the outer stick is in basic position on the index finger, and the inner stick is oriented to the thumb above the first joint. Practice going back and forth between the intervals of a second and third. Don't play the next one until your hand is set. Keep thinking: interval of a second = special position with straightened, pointing 2nd finger and tip of thumb hooked between the mallets—then, play it. *Then*, interval of a third = basic position (albeit a slightly cramped version)—then, play it; and keep repeating this.

STEP 9: Catching up the other hand

Review STEP 7, concentrating on your other hand. Start with an interval of a fourth: for instance, G and C. Keep the inside mallet on the C and gradually open out with the outer mallet (2nd finger) as well as with the thumb (as described in STEP 7).

Also review STEP 8, focusing on your other hand.

STEP 10: Mallet independence/outer mallet

The final basic component involves understanding how to use the mallets independently. First, we'll address how the outer mallets (1 and 4) function.

Stand squarely in front of the middle of the marimba. Holding both mallets in your right hand, extend your right arm out to the side, so that mallet 4 (the outer mallet in your right hand) is resting on a high note. I've suggested an exaggerated reach to accentuate the fundamentals of how you will use this mallet.

From this position, turn your head to the right so that you can look over your shoulder to see the length of your arm. Imagine drawing a line from your shoulder down your arm and, from your wrist, continuing straight along the tendon to the knuckle of your 2nd finger, and down the 2nd finger, with which the mallet is aligned, to the mallet shaft and, finally, the mallet head.

Now raise the mallet with the wrist (using the same type of motion as with matched-grip snare drum playing), and play with mallet 4. Imagine that the knuckle of the 2nd finger is triggering each stroke, or that the 2nd knuckle and finger is *pointing* in the direction of each downstroke. Mallet 4 works from the same wrist motion you used to play simple double-stops in STEP 4. The top of your hand should be as flat as possible, rather than rotated with your thumb above your hand, with the inside corner of your wrist (below the thumb) tilting down and inward. See Photo 12.

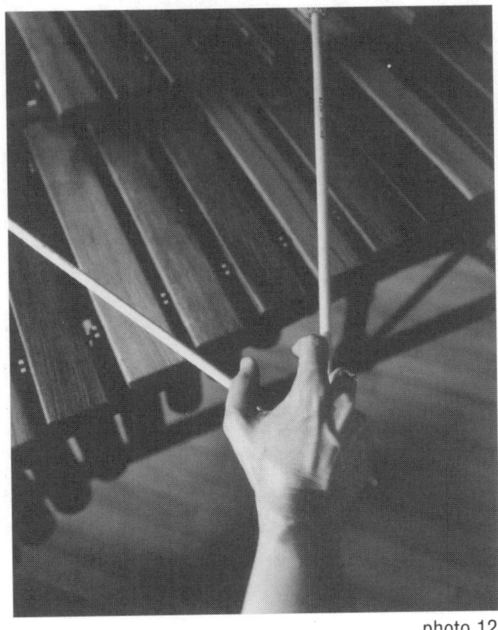

photo 12

Play some slow, single strokes on one note at *mf*. The same power that you discovered in STEP 5 is available from the wrist, even using low strokes, is applicable to both outer mallets (1 and 4).

If you have difficulty keeping mallet 3 from striking extraneous keys as you're playing with mallet 4, try holding the head of mallet 3 in the air (with your free hand) as you play with mallet 4. (While trying this, the mallet handles will be related in a + configuration.) This will enable you to see that, when it is used independently, mallet 4 can pivot off a fairly stationary mallet 3. Figure out some minor finger-repositionings "underneath" so that, when your free hand stops holding the head of mallet 3, that mallet remains stationary. The secret will probably be to squeeze with the 5th finger (and maybe also with the 4th finger) to keep the temporarily unwanted mallet (3) out of the way.

STEP 11: Mallet independence/inner mallet

The stroke is different for the inner mallets, numbers 2 and 3. The power for single strokes with the inner mallets will come from your thumb. With the inner mallets, your stroke *will* involve some wrist rotation. Here, again, there is an exaggerated movement for you to try—one-time only—to get the feel of this stroke.

Holding both mallets in your dominant hand, but aiming to play only with the inner mallet, try a crazy stroke beginning with your wrist rotated so extremely (outward) that your fingers are facing up! Now, quickly flop your hand over, letting the mallet head hit whatever note(s) it lands on. This reveals the tremendous power you have at the base of the thumb. You will see that this power also exists coming off much more subtle wrist rotations. See Photo 13.

photo 13

Play some slow, repeated strokes on one note at *mf* with the inner mallet. If you find that the outer mallet is flopping onto extraneous keys while you're trying to play only with the inner mallet, reach across with your free hand to hold the head of the outer mallet while you play with the inner mallet. You will feel that the inner mallet can pivot off the outer mallet and that, with some subtle changes of finger positions underneath, you can keep the outer mallet raised and out of the way while the inner mallet plays independently.

So, subtle snaps from the base of the thumb will trigger the inner mallets. Because of the slight rotation motion, it is slightly more challenging to play accurately directed notes with the inner mallets (2 and 3) than with the outer mallets. Try to give extra attention to clearly directed inner-mallet strokes as you practice.

STEP 12: Catching up the other hand

Repeat STEPS 10 and 11 to work on independent strokes with your other hand. Then practice some symmetrical strokes alternated between your hands to reinforce in which manner they operate independently; that is, mallets 1 and 4 (downstrokes), and mallets 2 and 3 (rotation stroke).

OVERVIEW 3

Through all of these steps, pay careful attention to whether one hand happens to initially feel more comfortable than the other. If so, try to figure out why and have the slower-learning hand copy it.

The final step, obviously, is to apply traditional grip to some actual playing. Play something with which you're already familiar, approaching it slowly, recalling the various steps—or, just try some scales.

There are many other nuances of traditional grip I could describe but, in general, I feel that slight variations in how people use their fingers is a natural component of the grip. To me, the beauty of the grip is that it allows for a number of subtle variations and still works. So, if any of these guidelines don't quite suit you, feel free to try minor alterations.

VIRTUES OF TRADITIONAL GRIP

1. Being slightly choked-up on the mallet handles, at a natural fulcrum, affords good leverage so that the mallet heads don't feel too top-heavy. We take the same approach to holding silverware or chopsticks.
2. The feeling of security inherent in holding the two mallets together at that fulcrum affords power. This is also true of Burton grip. In contrast, many players using an independent-mallet-grip—particularly younger players, or those with small or slender hands—find it difficult to build the adequate strength with which to be able to play loudly.

3. Most people find it easier to hold heavier mallets with one of the cross-grips than with the independent-mallet grips. In general, light-weight mallets tend to produce a thin tone. You will discover that it can be particularly effective to use heavier mallets in your left hand to improve the tone you produce from the bass notes.
4. Because you can vary how choked-up you are on the mallet handles, certain moves will be much easier. For example, take a one-handed roll on one note. With traditional grip, your elbow doesn't need to be nearly as extended as it does with Stevens grip. With the latter grip, a player must cope with the full extension of the mallets held at the ends. The contorted movements that can result sometimes distract from the music.
5. With traditional grip, because you can easily vary your finger pressure on the mallet handles, it is easier to vary articulations. With the other grips, the nature of how you are holding the mallets means you are hemmed into more actual gripping. The other side of the coin is that the "gripping" of Musser and Stevens grips, in particular, does enable more controlled, articulate triggering of independent mallets than can easily be achieved with traditional grip. However, for me, the expressive possibilities gained from the former don't outweigh the latter.
6. While Burton grip shares with traditional grip advantages numbers 1, 2, 3, and 4 above, it is difficult for some players to achieve number 5 with Burton grip. In comparison to traditional grip, it is also more difficult with Burton grip for most players to reach wide intervals and to keep the mallet handles from clicking together. It is understandable that Burton grip is extremely popular with vibraphonists, as it affords tremendous power (often necessary to compete with the volume of a band situation) on an instrument where extremely wide interval reaches are called for much less frequently than on marimba. But, generally, traditional grip can offer almost as much power.

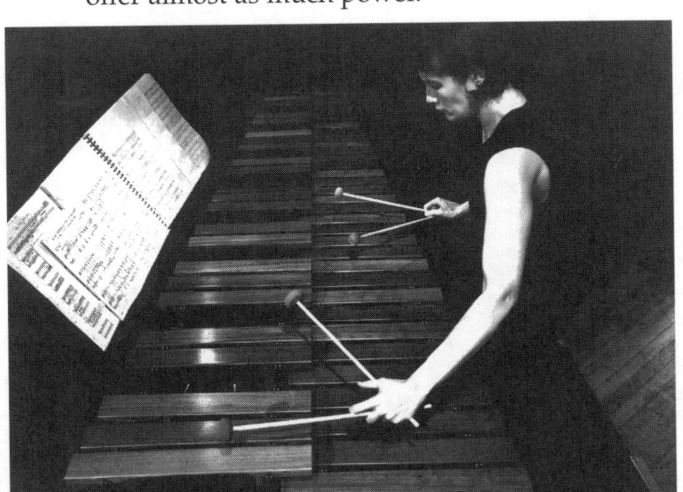

1C Basic Beating Spots

The best-sounding spot on each bar is the exact center (of the length) of the bar, right over the resonator. On the natural bank of bars (that is, the "white keys," if we make an analogy between the piano keyboard and the marimba), these are fairly easy targets, since they are close to us. On the sharp/flat bars (or "black keys"), the center of the bar can sometimes be an awkward target, especially in the context of a fast-moving line or in a chordal passage involving both a "white" and "black" note to be played by the same hand. Such situations often require a strained wrist angle, and aiming for the center of the "black" note can make things even more difficult.

The second-best sounding spot on each bar is the very end of the bar—*the edge*. Sometimes I almost aim for this at a diagonal angle. It's important not to get lazy when you're aiming for the end of the bar because very close to the edge, is the nodal point—the worst sounding spot on each bar. (The "node" is where the string goes through the bar.)

So, for much of my playing, I aim for the center of the "white" keys and the edge of the "black" keys. This approach affords your playing a look of ease and fluidity. I "go the extra distance" to play the center of the "black" keys whenever I want a slightly fuller, more resonant tone than is possible when playing on the edge, and whenever there is plenty of time to get to the center.

Your goal should be to always aim for these preferred beating spots. It should become ingrained that, whenever you're going for a certain note, you're also headed for a prime, chosen beating spot. Don't be satisfied with just hitting the correct note. Consider the precision required of string players to finger a note in tune. That should inspire us to aim for a precise spot the size of a half-dollar. Achieving consistency in your beating spots is the first step toward playing with a consistent, quality tone. (We will return to the subject of beating spots in Section III–A: Refining Strokes and Tone Production.)

1D Basic Strokes and Tone Production

Plunking a mallet down on the marimba to make a sound is very easy. In spite of this, almost everyone *can* produce a special, individual tone. Therefore, even beginning marimbists should learn some basic principles of sound production in order to distinguish themselves from total novices.

The main factors that contribute to your tone are:

1. how tightly or loosely you hold the mallet;
2. the height from which you strike the bar;
3. how you come off the bar after making contact;
4. the speed of your downstroke;
5. the speed of your upstroke.

I always strive to play with a full tone. A full tone can be achieved at all dynamic levels. In Section I-B, Step 4, I mentioned my preference for strokes remaining quite low to the keyboard and using wrist snap to achieve power and volume. I'll now describe in detail my basic stroke, which I believe achieves the fullest tone. Apply this to single, repeated strokes on one note, or to playing a slow scale (concentrating on the tone of each note), either with one mallet or with slow strokes alternating between hands. Play at a dynamic level of ***mf***.

The stroke begins fairly low to the bar and feels as if it's directed deeply into the bar. In order to play as loud as ***mf*** or beyond, you will be applying some wrist snap. I imagine that I'm not just trying to hit the surface of the bar but, rather, that the mallet head is continuing down through the surface of the bar, attempting to scoop out more sound that lies an eighth-of-an-inch under the surface of the bar. So, it is an extremely downward-oriented stroke.

After making contact, I purposefully stop the mallet about a half-inch above the surface of the bar. After the momentum of the downstroke, stopping the mallet at this point requires some tensing of your wrist muscles. In doing so—and, to be clear, this is taking place *after* I made contact with the bar—I have the image that I am actively *trapping* the resonance of that bar with the mallet head. Acoustically, I believe there may actually be something to this; the "trapped" soundwaves are causing the note to sound fuller because they are bouncing between the end of the resonator column and the mallet head. This basic stroke achieves a full sound; it could also be described as a "tenuto" stroke. In contrast, if, after the point of contact, you lift your mallet head very quickly off the bar, you will hear a thinner, more airy sound.

Upstrokes have been widely taught. Many players strive for each stroke to begin and end at the same medium-high reference point. There is no doubt that this results in a consistent, particular tone. But, to my ear, it is a less full tone than is produced by playing into the bar. Strokes that start and finish in the same point in the air generally have more of an upstroke, rather than a downstroke, feeling. If you are predominantly oriented to downstrokes, you will have more leverage from which to vary your strokes in order to achieve different articulations.

Many expressive nuances can be achieved by expanding on the basic stroke I described. They are controlled by the same factors that are listed above as fundamental components of sound production. I will discuss articulations in more depth in Section III-A: Refining Strokes and Tone Production.

Having emphasized low strokes, I should also acknowledge the correlation between stroke height and volume. Of course, higher strokes enable you to play louder; conversely, it's easy to play softly using very low strokes. And I *do* often use fairly high strokes to play loudly. But I am conscious of using arm as well as wrist motions, which play a part in my control of the tone. If you only use height to achieve volume, you run the risk of producing a somewhat "slappy," thin sound, and even more so if your downstroke is very fast.

1E Basics of Four-Mallet Stickings

Managing four mallets may seem difficult at first, especially if you are accustomed to playing with just two mallets or sticks, but once you get used to four mallets, you will find that they can help you get around more easily in many circumstances. When I play with two mallets, I generally hold them in an inverted "V" position—visualizing the tip of the V as two mallet heads on the same note, or neighboring notes. When holding four mallets, my inner mallets are in a similar V position. My outer mallets are poised to play notes in the outer reaches in either direction.

The most important guideline for deciding on four-mallet stickings is to always recognize which mallets can be used in order for you to move around as little as possible. One scenario in which you could use four mallets to minimize movement would be if you were playing a single line with the two inner mallets, and then used an outer mallet to cover a wide intervalic leap (see Section II, Study 4, m. 4). Use common sense; if you need to play a very high note, it will almost always be with mallet 4. A low note will almost always be played with mallet 1.

With traditional grip, I feel that my strongest mallets are numbers 1 and 4, so I am very comfortable using them as outer extensions. This complements the fact that bass and soprano notes (or lines) frequently require emphasis. (Stevens or Musser Grip users tend to favor their inner mallets, often, for example, leading with mallet 3 on high notes or passages. This means they are not taking advantage of the natural arm extensions available from the outer mallets, and their body movements are more exaggerated than necessary.)

When playing single-line passages (including scales), I commonly use mallets 2 and 4 (especially in the high range), keeping mallet 3 in near my stomach. This is particularly comfortable when a line is moving upward, because I know I will be utilizing the fullest possible extension when the highest notes are played with mallet 4. Musically, I will be leading with one of my strong mallets toward what may well be the peak of the phrase line. (The latter is true in the "Prélude" of the first Bach cello suite included in Section III-B: Relationship of Sticking Choices to Phrasing, mm. 37 and 38, leading to the downbeat of m. 39.)

In the middle register, I could use the latter sticking or switch to mallets 2 and 3 (the inner mallets). Those are the most common sticking combinations, but I occasionally use mallets 1 and 3 so that, when I go very low, I have mallet 1 ready to emphasize important bass notes. (Study 32 in Section II explores this sticking combination.) In scalar playing, sometimes a good point in which to switch combinations of mallets can be coming off "black" keys onto "white" keys, or the opposite.

Another good basic is to play double-stops, whenever possible, with the two mallets of one hand rather than with one mallet from each hand. This will probably eliminate the problem of playing flams (two notes not hitting exactly together). Also, whenever there are two notes in a row on the same pitch(es), the phrasing will generally sound best if they are played in the same hand. For other sticking basics that tie into phrasing, see Section I-J. Basics of Good Phrasing.

Since I frequently use graduated mallets (incrementally different mallets, from a softer one in the bass to a harder one in the 4 position), I will discuss briefly how these relate to sticking considerations. I feel that, generally, if you need to cover a wide range of the marimba, using graduated mallets can improve the quality of tone you achieve in different registers. (More will be said on this in Section III– E. Refining Mallet Selection.)

For a piece using mostly the middle of the marimba, with a little bit of high playing and a bit more low playing, I might choose a graduated combination such as Encore NZ mallets (from left to right): NZ5, NZ4, NZ3, NZ2. There are subtle differences between each successive mallet. This combination would work best if most of the playing was in left-hand and right-hand double-stops. But, if there was also some single-line playing with mallets 2 and 3, you could mitigate the difference between them by holding mallet 2 (the NZ4) in a "pinched" or clenched fashion, and holding mallet 3 (the NZ3) rather loosely.

For passages that went higher, it might be tricky to play with mallets 2 and 4 (as, with the aforementioned combination of mallets, you'd be playing with an NZ4 and NZ2), but you could be successful for a short period by exaggerating the same concept. If you had some single-line playing that went low, it would work well to use mallets 1 and 3—holding 1 tightly and 3 loosely—which would probably also add clarity to a low scale passage. You would then have mallet 1 ready if the music suddenly called for some fuller bass playing, for which you could return to a fuller-sounding stroke with that mallet.

Scales

Practicing scales is very useful for getting your hands moving and alternating smoothly. (You don't want to sound right- or left-hand heavy.) Scales are also a good introduction to music theory. Each note within a given octave can be a "key" center. Studying scales will help you get comfortable with all the keys, as well as the character of various types of scales. (The major and minor scales are the most important ones to know.)

There are many books in which scales are written out, so I am not going to take the space to do that. Instead, I will provide the basic information from which you will be able to figure them out for yourself. You can write them out in every key if you wish, or just memorize them.

Scales are played alternating between one mallet in each hand. They are frequently played with just two mallets, but if you wish, you can continue to hold four mallets as you play scales. With two mallets in each hand, you have a choice of *which* mallet you use from either hand (see the previous chapter). The most common combinations are mallets 2 and 3, or 2 and 4.

Scales are generally performed in the middle and high register of the marimba as opposed to the low register, where they can sound muddy. I recommend practicing them in an even rhythm (that is, notes evenly spaced in time), ascending from the tonic note, traversing two or three octaves, descending immediately from the top tonic note, and ending on the same note on which you started.

Scale practice is an excellent time to pay special attention to ideal beating spots. I suggest you target the middle of the "white" keys and the edge of the "black" keys. Try to play with a full, confident tone.

In playing major or minor scales, you will notice that if you cover an uneven number of octaves (one or three), you will reach the top note with the opposite hand you started with. Conversely, when you play them an even number of octaves (two or four), you will reach the top note with the same hand you started with. I like to plan ahead so that my right hand (the hand which most naturally extends to the high end of the instruments) plays the top note. Therefore, when I play scales covering two octaves, I start with the right hand. When I play them three octaves, I start with the left hand. Practicing them over two or three octaves is most common.

Avoid crossing your mallets as you play scales; instead you can shift one hand out of the way of the other. For example, if you are going to play a B-flat major scale (in which the first few notes are B-flat, C, D) beginning with the right hand, don't begin with your right hand crossed over your left; you want to keep your mallet heads untangled. Instead, begin by having your right mallet poised over the edge of the B-flat and the left mallet hovering to the left of it. After you play the B-flat with the right mallet head, shift it to the right toward the next note it will play (D); then the left hand can easily move to the C.

In playing scales that span several octaves, your body should freely move sideways across the expanse of the instrument; don't hesitate to take side steps to the right and left, with some foot crosses thrown in. You don't want to make a big deal about moving, but neither do you want to be lead-footed and having to lean to the sides. Ideally, try to walk a little bit ahead of your hands, so that your feet are always enabling that inverted "V" position of your inner mallets (discussed in the previous chapter) to be in front of your torso.

Once you understand the scales from a theoretical point of view, use them as a means toward getting more comfortable with the keyboard visually. Try to memorize how each scale *looks* against the pattern of "white" and "black" notes.

Besides practicing scales over a certain number of octaves, it can also be helpful to practice them the entire range of your instrument. This prepares you for the fact that, when scales arise is a piece of music, they rarely begin and end on the tonic. It also serves to further ingrain the visual patterns of different scales. For example, play a B-flat major scale beginning on low C if you have a 5-octave marimba, or on the low A if you have a 4-1/3-octave instrument, and play all the way up to the marimba's top note, C, before descending/returning to the lowest note. In so doing, you have covered every note on your instrument within the B-flat major scale.

For scales across the entire keyboard, you could either use mallets 2 and 3, or 2 and 4, the entire way. Or it's possible to mix stickings. First, visualize a rough division of your marimba into thirds. You could play the lowest third of the instrument with mallets 1 and 3, the middle third of the instrument with mallets 2 and 3, and the top third of the instrument with mallets 2 and 4 (so that you're integrating mallets 1 and 4 to play notes in the outer extensions: very low, or very high). Mixing stickings isn't necessarily better than using the same one the whole time, but it's worth trying. Ultimately, use what you find most comfortable.

Regarding the tempo for practicing scales, I recommend a minimum speed of eighth notes played at quarter note = 100. The optimum speed is probably sixteenth notes at quarter note = 120. But, don't try to play them that fast until you're ready. It's more important that you play them accurately with good form, beating spots, and tone.

Chromatic Scales

These can start on any note and require you to play every single note, moving by half steps, ascending and then descending. Chromatic scales are usually played either starting and ending on the same note, or the entire range of your instrument. It's unnecessary to practice chromatic scales beginning on each successive starting note within an octave, as they are pretty much all the same. (The only difference is which hand plays the set of two and three black notes first.)

The Circle of Fifths (or Fourths)

Each of the following scales can be played in every key. Since there are twelve notes in a chromatic scale, we can relate them to a clock face (which, of course, has twelve numbers). We could arbitrarily re-label 12:00 as "C." Then replace all the numbers with the following key centers: 1 = G, 2 = D, 3 = A, 4 = E/F-flat, 5 = B/C-flat, 6 = F-sharp/G-flat, 7 = C-sharp/D-flat, 8 = G-sharp/A-flat, 9 = D-sharp/E-flat, 10 = A-sharp/B-flat, 11 = E-sharp/F. 12:00 (with C) can also be labeled B-sharp. You have now assigned every note within an octave a place on the clock circle.

Perhaps you noticed that each successive re-labeling of the numbers was a note an interval of a fifth higher than the previous one. If you went counter-clockwise from C, each successive re-labeled number is a note an interval of a fifth lower (or fourth higher) than the previous one. This is called "the circle of fifths." (An interesting symmetry is that all the pitches that lay directly across from one another on the clock, for instance 2=D and 8=A-flat, are a tritone apart.)

Sharps and Flats

Except for the keys of C major and A minor, which have no sharps or flats in their key signatures, every other major and minor scale has a key signature that has between one and seven sharps or flats. Increasing numbers of sharps and flats always appear in the same order and are always notated on the same place on the staff, as follows:

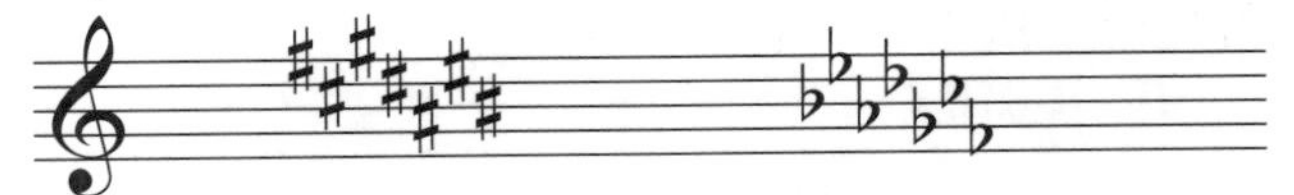

It is interesting that they, too, follow the circle of fifths. If you start with F-sharp (at 6:00) and move clockwise, you find the names of the other six sharps. The seven names of the flats appear starting with B-flat (10:00) and continuing counter-clockwise. It is also interesting to note that the letter names of the sharps in order—F, C, G, D, A, E, B—is the reverse order of the flats.

Major Scales

Major scales consist of the following intervals: whole step, whole step, half step, whole step, whole step, whole step and half step—or W, W, H, W, W, W, H. The key signatures for each scale ensure that you will play that configuration of whole and half steps. First, there's C with no sharps or flats.

The scales with sharps are:

- **G major**—one sharp (F-sharp)
- **D major**—two sharps (F-sharp and C-sharp)
- **A major**—with three sharps (F-sharp, C-sharp and G-sharp)
- **E major**—four sharps (F-sharp, C-sharp, G-sharp and D-sharp)
- **B major**—five sharps (F-sharp, C-sharp, G-sharp, D-sharp and A-sharp)
- **F-sharp major**—six sharps (F-sharp, C-sharp, G-sharp, D-sharp, A-sharp and E-sharp)
- **C-sharp major**—seven sharps (F-sharp, C-sharp, G-sharp, D-sharp, A-sharp, E-sharp and B-sharp)

The scales with flats are:

- **F major**—one flat (B-flat)
- **B-flat major**—two flats (B-flat and E-flat)
- **E-flat major**—three flats (B-flat, E-flat and A-flat)
- **A-flat major**—four flats (B-flat, E-flat, A-flat, and D-flat)
- **D-flat major**—five flats (B-flat, E-flat, A-flat, D-flat and G-flat)
- **G-flat major**—six flats (B-flat, E-flat, A-flat, D-flat, G-flat and C-flat)
- **C-flat major**—seven flats (B-flat, E-flat, A-flat, D-flat, G-flat, C-flat and F-flat)

Note that the last three scales on each of the above lists are actually the same, in reverse order; that is, B major is the same as C-flat, F-sharp is the same as G-flat, C-sharp is the same as D-flat. These keys are said to be "enharmonically" equivalent, which simply means that the notes are the same but they are "spelled" differently.

Minor Scales

All minor keys are related to a major key, meaning they have the same key signature as a particular major key. The "tonic" note of each relative major key is found an interval of a minor third higher than the tonic note of the minor key. There are three types of minor scales: natural minor, harmonic minor, and melodic minor. Each of the A minor scales, for example, is a "relative minor" of C major.

Natural minor scales—with an intervalic make-up of W, H, W, W, H, W, W—consist of exactly the same notes as the relative major scales, but they start on the relative minor tonic note. In other words, they simply follow the key signatures. It is common for all these forms of minor scales to be used to create a sense of minor tonality.

A natural minor—no sharps or flats
E natural minor—one sharp
B natural minor—two sharps
F-sharp natural minor—three sharps
C-sharp natural minor—four sharps
(G-sharp or) A-flat natural minor—(five sharps or) seven flats
(D-sharp or) E-flat natural minor—(six sharps or) six flats
(A-sharp or) B-flat natural minor—(seven sharps or) five flats
F natural minor—four flats
C natural minor—three flats
G natural minor—two flats
D natural minor—one flat

Harmonic minor scales have the same key signatures, but they have a raised seventh scale degree. Therefore, the notes in the scale of G melodic minor, for example, would be: G, A, B-flat, C, D, E-flat, F-sharp, G. The intervalic make-up of harmonic minor scales is: W, H, W, W, H, augmented second, H. The harmonic minor scales have a very distinctive character because of that augmented second; I think of them as sort of exotic-sounding. To write them, place the key signature at the beginning of the line and add the necessary sharp or natural sign immediately preceding the seventh note.

Melodic minor scales are the only scales that are different when ascending than descending. They are still written with the same key signatures. However, on the ascent, they have raised sixth and seventh scale degrees. The ascent of a C melodic minor scale, for example, would be: C, D, E-flat, F, G, A, B, C. (Notice this is identical to C major, except with the minor third, E-flat, instead of the major third). In writing this on a staff with a key signature, you would need to give the A and B natural signs. The intervalic make-up is: W, H, W, W, W, W, H. On the descent of the melodic minor scale, the sixth and seventh scale degrees are lowered so that they are simply played within the key signature. Therefore, the notes in the descending C melodic minor scale would be C, B-flat, A-flat, G, F, E-flat, D, and C (or exactly the same as the natural minor scale). In writing out the descent, you would need to reinstate the flats on the Bs and As.

Other Recommended Scales

Diminished Scales

These are also known as "octatonic scales" because they have eight rather than seven notes per octave. The intervalic pattern is either W, H, W, H, W, H, W, H or H, W, H, W, H, W, H, W—starting on each chromatic note. There are three different diminished scales. To chart this, I will arbitrarily call them diminished scale 1, 2 and 3. (For the sake of simplicity, I have omitted enharmonic spellings):

Starting note	W, H, W...	H, W, H...
C	1	2
C-sharp	2	3
D	3	1
E-flat	1	2
E	2	3
F	3	1
F-sharp	1	2
G	2	3
A-flat	3	1
A	1	2
B-flat	2	3
B	3	1

1: C, D, E-flat, F, F-sharp, G-sharp, A, B
2: C, C-sharp, D-sharp, E, F-sharp, G, A, A-flat, B-flat
3: C-sharp, D, E, F, G, A-flat, B-flat, B-natural

Whole-Tone Scales

The intervalic pattern for these is, as you might guess: W, W, W, W, W, W. Note that there are only six notes in this scale. You can practice these starting on each chromatic note. There are really only two different whole-tone scales (again, my numbering is arbitrary):
1: C, D, E, F-sharp, G-sharp, A-sharp
2: D-flat, E-flat, F, G, A, B

1G Basic Rolls

Many beginners on marimba already have some percussion experience. If you studied snare drum, you know that the goal when rolling on that instrument is to have an extremely fast, very even roll, usually by means of alternating double strokes (LLRR etc.) or multiple-bounce strokes. Marimba rolls don't generally need to be very fast, and they are played using alternating single strokes (LRLR etc.) like timpani rolls.

The nature of percussion instruments is that, once a note is struck, it resonates. The length of the resonance will vary from extremely short (as in the case of a snare drum note) to quite long (as in the case of a timpani or low marimba note). The attack is usually significantly louder than the resonance which follows. Rolls, therefore, are used on percussion instruments for two main reasons: (1) to extend the duration of the note; and (2) to enable dynamic control of the sustained note.

However, in relation to long notes sung by a vocalist or played on instruments using breath or long bow strokes, rolls on percussion instruments add a special—if not peculiar—texture to long-duration notes. In the former cases, the sustain is smooth. With percussion, it has an added "brrrrrrrrrrrr" (that's a rolled "r"!). Sometimes that texture is a nice addition; sometimes it isn't. The reality is that it usually has more in common with special effects used on certain instruments—for example, flutter-tonguing on flute, or tremoloing on violin—than with a normal sustained note on those instruments.

Roll Speed

If you've played timpani, it will be helpful to recall what happens when you roll on a note that is a relatively low pitch for a given kettle. When the head is quite loose, you can feel the waves of vibration that pass across it in reaction to the first note played. Generally, it's necessary to find a roll speed—probably quite slow—that doesn't "fight" the vibrations too much.

The same is true of a low marimba note. Try this experiment: With one hand, strike one of the lowest notes on your marimba with a very large marimba mallet, producing a big, resonant tone; really get the bar vibrating. With the other hand, hold a lighter, rather hard mallet just above the surface of the bar. Hold it very loosely and let it "catch" the vibration set off by the big, booming mallet. You are likely to catch a few bounces that are surprisingly slow (that is, wide apart). The distance between those bounces suggests how slowly you could roll on that note in order not to interrupt its natural vibrations/resonance.

This phenomenon leads to the following conclusion. In general, on marimba, it's best to roll rather slowly on low notes, at a medium speed in the middle register, and quite fast in the high register. This acknowledges the natural length of resonance in different registers. We can roll slower in the low register because the resonance is naturally long and full; we need to play a fast roll in the upper register because the natural resonance is short.

When you are thoughtful about the speed of your rolls, you can emphasize the smooth sustaining quality over the broken ("brrrrrrrrrrr") effect. It usually relates to finding a speed for your strokes that doesn't fight the note's resonance/vibrations. Other times, you may wish to accentuate the roll texture. I really believe you can alter the sound quality and effect of your rolls just by *imagining* how you would like them to sound! Your stroke will make subtle adjustments.

Expression

I want to get you thinking about the expressive possibilities inherent in rolls. I like to imagine that rolls are my *vibrato*. Despite the fact that vibrato (applied to voice or any wind or string instruments) technically refers to a wavering of pitch, I think we can emulate the texture and effect of vibrato, even though we are playing the same pitch. One way to achieve this is by varying the speeds of our rolls—as we would if we were singing.

Have you ever heard a jazz saxophonist come to the end of a ballad? As he fades out on a note, you gradually become more aware of his breath, and even certain "beautiful imperfections"—like a catch in his throat. I am not sure how this would translate to the marimba but I think it's a good example of how there can be beauty—"humanness"—in *un*evenness.

You need to develop an even roll on marimba. If you've had previous drumming experience, chances are you may easily bring to the marimba an intense, rapid-fire, even roll. If this describes you, relax! If you are just learning to roll, practice an even single-stroke roll at different steady speeds. You should be equally comfortable beginning with either hand.

But also experiment with ways in which slight variations in speed can be expressive, especially in the context of a piece. Consider taking a lot of liberties with your rolls. They do not always need to be even. Marimba is different and more forgiving than most other percussion instruments because of the singing nature of the resonance across most of the instrument.

Some of the most natural devices for making your rolls more expressive are: (1) increasing the speed of your roll to enhance a crescendo, (2) relaxing the speed to enhance a diminuendo, (3) rolling faster on louder notes, and (4) rolling slower on softer notes. Be thoughtful about how you apply these techniques to keep variety in your playing and to avoid predictability. The best way to get ideas about how to vary your rolls (in order to shape phrases) is to literally *sing* a passage, and take note of how you would apply vibrato (as well as how your throat feels; more on this in Section I-J: Basics of Good Phrasing).

Types of Four-Mallet Rolls

Most of what I've said so far relates to rolls in two-mallet playing, but much of it could be applied to four-mallet playing. In addition, there are two basic types of four-mallet rolls:

1. "2+2": alternated strokes between hands in which the two mallets in each hand hit simultaneously.
2. Ripple: alternated strokes between hands in which the two mallets in each hand do not hit simultaneously. Rather, they "flam," resulting in all four notes hitting at different times.

Personally, I almost always use the ripple roll. To me, when all the notes hit separately the end result sounds most homogenous. (To be perfectly honest, many people who predominantly use the "2+2" roll sound absolutely fine to me; I personally just can't accept the concept of taking a four-note chord and arbitrarily "distorting" it into two notes plus two notes.) Ripple rolls sound particularly beautiful in the upper register. With the same speed of alternations between hands, they can give the impression of being faster and, therefore, sound more legato.

When I do a ripple roll, my mallet heads drop in the following order: 4, 3, 1, 2 (or 1, 2, 4, 3; same thing). But, to learn it, I never drilled practicing that configuration of notes. I mainly thought of it as a "2+2 roll with flams."

To learn to ripple roll, I recommend you start out by playing a "2+2" roll very slowly. Gradually tilt your hands slightly outward so that the lower mallet naturally strikes first. Important: Do not add in any type of deliberate wrist rotation between the two notes of one hand in order to achieve the flam. Get the flam by playing a simple downstroke in which the outer mallet hits first.

When you are able to play alternating flams, gradually speed up the alternations of your hands until they are quite fast. There is one final trick to getting the roll to coalesce, which is a phenomenon I call "lift-off"—as in when an airplane takes off. If you can do fast flam alternations, a problem may be that they have too much of a down-stroke or dead-stroke sound. To whip them into a beautiful circular pattern in that configuration of notes, I do a tiny lift in my wrist so that the strokes take on an airier quality. (This results in tiny, clockwise circular patterns in mallet heads 1 and 2, and tiny counter-clockwise circular patterns in mallet heads 3 and 4.)

In addition to practicing the ripple roll as I just described, it will also work to practice your "2+2" roll at normal speed, and try to mess it up a bit! This is just another way to approach it. Sometimes it's very helpful to practice a new technique from a couple different approaches.

I really like the configuration of ripple roll described above; the outer mallets hitting first means it's easiest to bring out the soprano and bass voices—which is more often necessary than bringing out the inner voices. That said, it's necessary to be able to emphasize *any* individual note within a roll. This can be achieved by slightly varying your finger pressure and/or leaning your hand slightly toward certain notes.

More variations on rolls will be mentioned in Section III-C: Refining Rolls.

Measured Rolls

Although you have quite a bit of flexibility regarding the speed and—with four mallets—the style of your rolls, you do need to learn to fill precise amounts of space with them. Some people have trouble with this at first, which is quite understandable. It can feel strange to keep track of a steady measurement of time (that is, the tempo and the number of beats a roll needs to fill) while performing an *un*measured act (the roll). Your goal should be to fill the indicated duration of time with the roll, and then end the roll at the last possible instant before the entrance of the next event. Sometimes you can even roll *into* the next event (meaning, end the roll on the next note); use your judgment.

If you really have trouble keeping track of a tempo while playing unmeasured rolls, you might try for a while to play measured rolls. That is, decide on a particular number of hand alternations which, at a given tempo, provides a pleasant-sounding roll speed on a particular note or series of notes. This will help you keep track of specific beats while rolling. Eventually, however, you should be able to roll at any speed and simultaneously keep track of tempo.

General Considerations

I feel very strongly that marimbists should not allow the listener to hear one hand begin first on any roll of two, three, or four notes that begins out of silence. Yes, rolls consist of hand-alternations, but we don't need to expose that fact. When a pianist or an orchestra plays a chord, we hear the entire chord begin at once—not the high notes and then the low notes. It is much better to first strike the notes together, and then slip into alternations.

If you are moving between rolls in a legato fashion, it sounds fine to just maintain alternations; no one will really hear that one hand is leading the other. You do, however, need to shift between rolls in a manner that clearly implies the tempo.

You are likely to come across marimba rolls notated in several different ways. The most common—which I believe should become the standard—is three slashes through the stem of a note or chord (or just above or below notes without stems). This includes notes of any duration, and always indicates an unmeasured roll (for example, see Section II, Study 34).

Another approach (seen in some older notation books) is to show rolls of two to four notes as two separate notes with three slashes in the space between them. (This type of notation can be seen in Section II, Study 47, m. 13.) This is quite confusing, as your eye is challenged to combine two note durations into one, and you can't readily see what notes get played together. (In Study 47, however, it makes sense because of the "slow to fast" effect I want, starting with the upper notes.)

1H Learning the Keyboard Layout

It's very important to get to know the layout of the marimba *by feel*. My fabulous teacher Ian Finkel really emphasized this—for which I have been forever grateful. He introduced the point by saying that clarinetists would look pretty ridiculous if they kept craning to look around the side of the clarinet to see where they'd placed their fingers.

Of course, it's a different story when marimbists need to traverse eight-and-a-half feet of keyboard without our fingertips ever coming in contact with any of it (we have those *mallets* in the way!). I'm not advocating *never* looking down at the keyboard, but I think we can at least go a long way toward learning the layout by feel. (Ian used to hold a book opened flat in the air just above my hands, moving it laterally so that I couldn't see them. It also ensured that my mallets remained close to the keyboard.)

Study the bar widths of your marimba; there are generally a few spots on each keyboard where the bar widths widen or narrow. It's helpful to have in mind roughly where these are. Begin with a piece in which there is stepwise movement, or movements in recurring small intervals. Try to gain confidence with these; then try music with larger intervallic skips. If there are some tricky shifts in a piece you're playing, try making an exercise out of doing the shift without looking initially, "freeze," then check out where you landed.

It's important to be constantly targeting the most desirable beating spots (see Section I, C. Basic Beating Spots). Eventually, when you become more comfortable with moving around the keyboard without looking at it, you also want to automatically move to ideal beating spots.

Begin to rely on your ear to notify you of wrong notes; you don't need to see notes to be sure you got them right. It should get so that you only need to see the note to check out the beating spot you landed on. You should eventually know that by ear, too.

Knowing the keyboard layout by feel is invaluable when it comes to sight-reading or performing with music. If you are fairly comfortable with the keyboard layout, then you don't need to take your eyes off the music as much. This eliminates one of the biggest fears inherent in reading: that you might lose your spot on the page.

Of course, it is enormously helpful if you are always able to use the same instrument or brand of instrument. Having to constantly readjust to different keyboard layouts can be discouraging. However, the more consideration you give to factors such as where the bar widths change on each instrument, and taking care with your beating spots, the more likely you are to be able to quickly make adjustments when necessary.

Improving your knowledge of the marimba keyboard by feel is, for many, a lifelong pursuit. It is gradually achieved simply by keeping aware of it as a goal. Ultimately, it is a central factor in feeling that you can "embrace" the marimba—that you have a physical connection and comfort with it.

11 Basics of Good Rhythm and "Feel"

It's extremely important to develop a sense of steady time. This means you can deeply feel a steady beat. If, when you listen to pop dance music, you can you tap your hand or foot exactly with the beat, you're off to a good start.

A metronome is a crucial tool for teaching yourself to internalize and deepen a steady sense of time (tempo) as you play. Any metronome will suffice initially, but the ideal one can subdivide sixteenth notes and triplets. At first, you want to make sure you are listening and reacting in time to the metronome; eventually, you want to feel you *know* where the beats are, with or without the metronome. You will, hopefully, sometime experience the phenomenon of playing with a metronome but ceasing to hear it because you are playing with it so precisely.

Besides being able to feel beats steadily, it is essential that you learn to subdivide beats with absolute accuracy. The main requirements are to be able to divide a beat in half or into fourths—both are called "duple" subdivisions; or into triplets—or "triple" subdivisions. (The terms duple and triple can also be applied to meters, or time signatures.)

I am indebted to my teacher Vic Firth for insisting I drill these subdivisions with a metronome. It has helped me immeasurably, nearly every day of my life. We mainly approached it on a snare drum pad using George Stone's book *Stick Control*, but you could accomplish the same objective applied to the marimba using the following exercise. My drills didn't include quintuplets, but I have since wished they had, so they're included here. Divisions of a beat into sextuplets (six notes) could fall into either duple or triple subdivisions, depending on whether you think of them as two groups of three notes or three groups of two notes. (They are not included in the exercises because they are just further subdivisions. I want you to get very clear on the basics first.)

I encourage you to practice the following exercises until you are easily able to play these figures keeping steady time, and able to easily shift between the rhythmic patterns. You may wish to repeat each measure several times. Then you could make a loop of two consecutive measures and repeat that a number of times. Alter where the loop starts, so that you are practicing all the various connections between patterns. Of course, you can also play the exercise as a whole, and repeat it. It is not sufficient to be able to play the rhythms "about right." They must be absolutely precision-perfect. If you're not sure whether or not they are perfect, they aren't! Play with alternating strokes, and practice starting with each hand. Make sure your hands sound matched. You can sometimes play the quarter notes with the same hand, if you practice them with both your right and left hands. You may also wish to invent some sticking patterns that include various double-stickings (as *Stick Control* does) but don't go too crazy; keep it to stickings you think you might apply in real life. Besides playing the rhythms correctly, the most important thing is that your tone is full and matched between your hands, regardless of your sticking.

For the most part, focus on playing these exercises on one note. You may also wish to make up simple patterns of different notes, but don't get too fancy; keep the emphasis on the rhythm. When you are playing on one note with alternating strokes between hands, aim for virtually the same beating spot with each mallet head. This will help to ensure that the tone you produce with either hand matches. Some people make the mistake of establishing different spots for each mallet head, in order to prevent them from accidentally hitting each other. You don't need to make this allowance. Keep your mallets rather low; after each one plays, get it out of the way so the next one can aim for the same (or nearly the same) spot.

Start at a tempo of quarter note = 80. Try gradually increasing your speed up to about quarter note = 120. Try also gradually decreasing speed until you get down to about quarter note = 50. Playing these exercises with absolute accuracy is more challenging the slower they get.

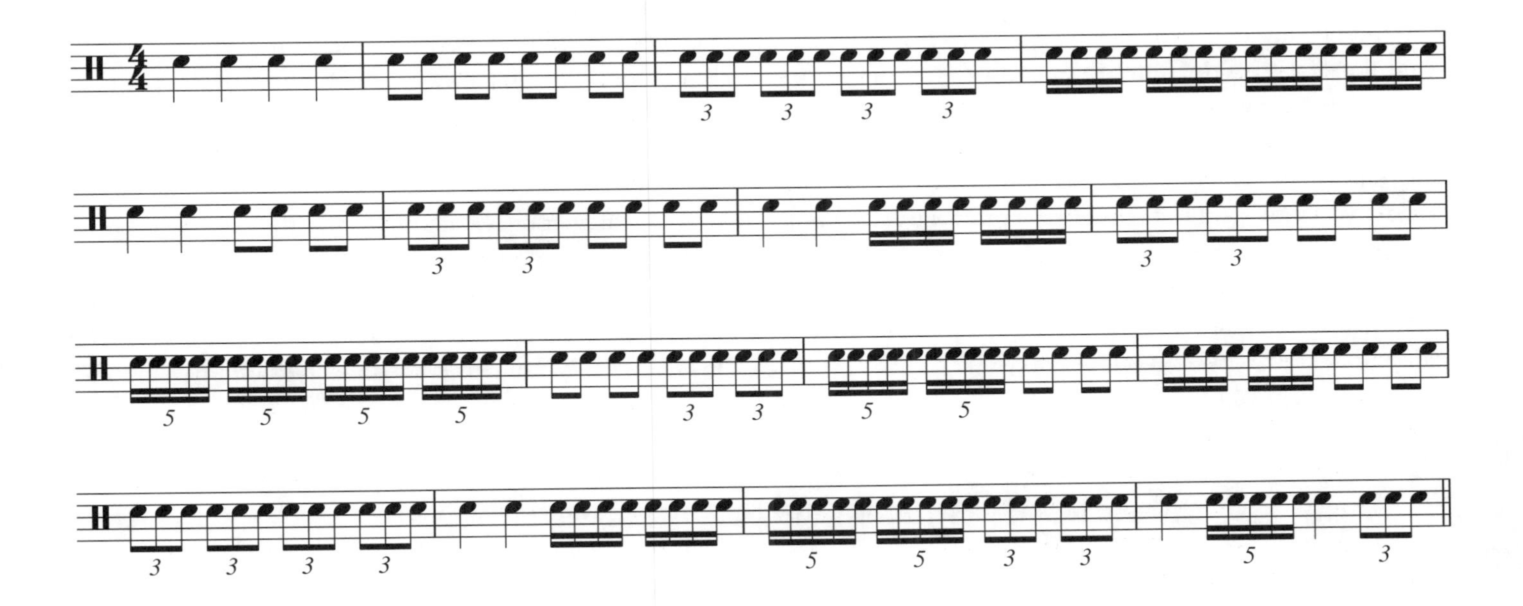

Natural accents are inherent in various meters. For example, in 4/4 time, the note that naturally receives the most stress is beat 1. Beat 3 receives the next-most stress. Beats 2 and 4 are both weaker. In 3/4 or 9/8 (felt in three main beats) or other triple meters, beat 1 receives the most stress, beat 2 receives the next-most stress, and beat 3 is the weakest. You may also wish to apply this additional layer of musical nuance to the given exercises. You will find that it is extremely important to consider with everything you play.

In addition to working with a metronome, I strongly advocate that players learn to very accurately tongue background rhythms in their mouths. By that I mean very deliberately bouncing your tongue to the roof of your mouth, as if you were whispering "Ta, ta, ta, ta" or "Da, da, da, da." This serves as an inner metronome. You can do it along with a metronome to practice internalizing steady tempos, or to further subdivide beats the metronome clicks out—especially in slow tempos. It requires a fair amount of practice to be able to rely on your tonguing even when you're having difficulty playing something at the same time. But if you can learn to evenly, reliably tongue—independent of what you are playing—it will absolutely change your life: guaranteed! (For an advanced application of tonguing techniques, see Section V, Tumblers, Performance Advice on Excerpt I.)

It can also be very helpful to learn to count out loud (that is, speak) while you practice. Again, you need to get it to the point that you can count steadily and accurately despite what your hands are playing. Being able to speak while you play is helpful with basic counting (such as: "One and two and three and one, etc.") but can really be invaluable when working on a piece in mixed meters (such as 3/4, 5/8, 3/16, 2/8, etc.) when it's more difficult to make use of a metronome.

Moreover, being able to count out loud is a fabulous coordination exercise that can relate to other situations in which you will need to think of two (or more) strands of information at once. For example, it has helped me to more easily keep track of two important lines occurring simultaneously in a piece of music (over which there could be additional strands of information, such as a crescendo, or a ritard). It has also helped me in playing chamber music to keep better track of what another person is playing.

Another good device for bringing steady rhythm into your body is foot tapping. It's one thing to mindlessly tap while you're enjoying a song with a good beat; it can be quite another thing to learn to tap so accurately that it can serve as another metronome. The heel of your foot should remain on the floor. Lift up the front of your foot and then purposeful tap it to meet the floor exactly on the beat. If you are playing duple rhythms, you can also raise your foot exactly in time so as to subdivide the beat in half, in which case it's at the "up" position exactly in the middle of your main beat. When you come across beats divided into triple rhythms, you would then *avoid* emphasizing the upbeat (up-foot) subdivision and, instead, rely on your knowledge of how to evenly divide a beat into three parts, as you drilled in the exercise given here.

Good rhythm, in many ways, stems from your whole body. In the course of explaining traditional grip, I recommended a basic posture (Step 4). Beyond this, I advocate trying to conserve motion as much as possible from the waist up (including your arms), and trying to feel as free as possible from the waist down. It helps to have an awareness of how you shift your weight from one hip to the other. As I mentioned in Section I-F. Scales, you can freely shift your weight between your feet, and walk from side to side. Feel loose from your hips. All of these elements tie together to supply a flexible but solid basis for all your movements, which can palpably affect how you feel rhythm.

So far, I have discussed good rhythm in terms of staying precisely with a metronome. When you do so, you are playing in what is also known as the "center" of the beat. It's also possible to keep a steady beat while playing just a fraction "on the back of the beat," and a fraction "in front of the beat." These are basic changes in "feel" that can have very interesting effects on your playing. Different styles of music, as well as particular pieces, can greatly benefit from your application of one of these approaches to keeping time.

Almost everyone has a natural tendency to feel tempo in one of these ways. This doesn't mean you will always play with that type of feel; it's just the one you most naturally gravitate toward. You need to concentrate a little harder to play within the others. Recognizing what category someone else leans toward can help you to play with that person in small settings because it indicates what types of adjustments you might need to make. (At an advanced or professional level, this is probably not something that would be discussed; players would just sense it.)

For instance, I tend to play in front of the beat. It means I often have to fight the tendency to rush. But I have also noticed that "front of the beat" players can have an exciting energy in their playing. "On the beat" players generally have the easiest time keeping steady time internally. "Back of the beat" players can have the effect of seeming very playful in a relaxed way. (One of the greatest "back of the beat" players is the drummer Elvin Jones.)

Elasticity of feel, combined with various types of articulations and phrasing (see next chapter), can be used to bring different attitudes or characters to your music; for example, "elegant," "cute," "reserved," "extroverted"—even "goofy." You can sometimes be quite flexible with the timing of notes for expressive effect.

This is to say you can sometimes play *un*evenly. "Rubato" means that you intentionally stretch or rush certain groups of notes. The secret to doing this tastefully and effectively is to always be subdividing rhythms in the background, or as a backdrop, to the passage you're playing. If your background subdivisions smoothly slow down or speed up, the written rhythms you're playing—relative to your background subdivisions—will usually sound quite natural and amount to a convincing, expressive rubato.

An example would be a brief cadence in a Bach fugue. The harmony will be clearest if you slow down a bit in order for the cadence to clearly be heard, but it can be easy to overdo this. If, for instance, while you play a few cadential quarter notes you continue to subdivide (in your mind, or in your mouth!) eighth notes that gradually slow down, they "will keep you in line" and prevent you from overdoing the ritard. If the eighth-note subdivisions quickly but smoothly gain speed after the resolution, they will provide a good framework for naturally regaining tempo. This way, the basic integrity of the rhythms and tempo remain intact.

1J Basics of Good Phrasing

In the music world, it's fairly common to hear it said that someone is "quite musical" or someone else is "*extremely* musical." "Musicality" is a pretty elusive concept. There are young players who have "it"—that is, musicality, or talent—even though "it" will continue to mature. I've heard it said that musicality cannot be taught; it's either there (in a musician) or it isn't. In my experience that's often true, but I have also seen cases in which players, given some guidance, succeeded in becoming more musical. In most cases, it meant they gained insights into phrasing.

"Interpretation" describes the way a musician makes sense of the basic elements of music: meter, rhythms, pitches, dynamics, and other directives. It requires imagination. But some people can be good interpreters—and, through that, show they are skilled musicians—yet not necessarily play really musically. The missing element in those cases is a sensitivity to phrasing possibilities.

In phrasing musically, you create a sort of sentence structure with sound. You shape the sentences so that their meaning is clearest and most persuasive. It means you are able to render the notes on a page (or notes in your mind) on an instrument (or with your voice) in a manner that combines the raw elements (pitches, rhythms, dynamics, etc.) with an abstract, artistic magic, which changes them into something that *communicates*—something that, like air, is elusively indescribable, yet perfect: Music!

My father (at age 93) lent me a cherished videotape of Vladimir Horowitz playing a recital in Moscow when Horowitz was 81 (Horowitz was born just four years before my father, and both spent their childhoods in Russia.) Pointing to the tape, my Dad leaned forward, smiling, and quietly, deliberately recommended to me, "Sometimes, close your eyes when you listen to it. He is absolutely *talking* to you." Indeed, Horowitz did.

Singers and players of wind instruments know intimately how crucially their breathing affects their phrasing. Since the rest of us also breathe and can sing (even if poorly!), we are perfectly capable of creating beautiful phrases too.

It's really important to continually imagine how you would sing melodic lines. Take notice of how you need to breathe in order to beautifully shape the line (even if your actual singing isn't beautiful!). Take notice of how you use your breath to support the key features of the melodic contours. Become aware of all the nuances of how it feels to sing across your vocal range: for example, the way your throat tightens when you reach to sing a high note, and the way you have to sink into your chest to produce a low note.

Try to translate those phenomena into your marimba playing. Key factors in accomplishing this will be nuances of touch, tone, and dynamics; attention to the speed and shape of rolls; and a sensitivity to subtle ways you can play with time—as in "feel" or actual rubato (slight increases or decreases in tempo for expressive purposes; see the end of the previous chapter).

Also use singing techniques to enhance rhythmic figures. For instance, if you need to play a kind of "groovy" or "funky" rhythm, make up some vocal technique—probably using all kinds of wild, percussive effects from your mouth—to vocalize the rhythm. You will probably discover that, in order to make it *really* "groovy," you are "ghosting" certain notes. ("Ghosting" notes means singing or playing them almost inaudibly so they are more "felt" than heard.) If you can translate that to the marimba, your marimba playing will be much groovier!

Generally, unless it is the feature of a particular piece, any two or more consecutive notes played at exactly the same dynamic and with the same tone quality will sound quite dull. The reason is that musical lines (phrases) are always "on their way somewhere" or "heading back from somewhere." So, it wouldn't make sense for there to be stagnation, unless it's for a particular effect. Always consider where lines are going and make that clear.

One phrasing technique that works beautifully on marimba is to imagine there is a "hairpin" diminuendo ($>$) beginning underneath the first note of every phrase and ending on the last note within the phrase mark (or slur). Play the diminuendo *very subtly*. The effect it will create is that the notes seem to blur together a little and, therefore, they seem phrased. When a phrase crescendos, it is still possible to show the beginning of the phrase by leaning on it a little, and to still give the impression of the phrase shaping through the use of dynamics.

I often try to imagine that a set of notes I am trying to phrase together all fall out of one arm movement. By this I mean that I try to make one heavy, weighted motion based at my shoulder. (You wouldn't be able to *see* that I am involving my shoulder; I would just feel that the gesture stems from there.) Of course, I am lifting up slightly after each stroke and actually playing separate downstrokes, but I try to minimize their separateness with this image of several of them coming from one larger motion. This helps the notes to seem more connected. More importantly, it provides relief from the constant vertical motions of your strokes by giving the impression of horizontal motions.

In the previous chapter I mentioned the natural accents inherent in various meters. These can play an important role in phrasing. For example, a triplet that appears in any kind of music should be recognizable as a triplet because of the relative weight of the notes in the group: strongest, next-strongest, weakest. So, the triplet would itself be phrased, and would possibly also exist within the context of a larger phrase structure.

Your choice of stickings can really influence your phrasing. My basic goal is to have what I call a "clean hand" ready to play any important note in a phrase. Usually, the most important notes are the beginnings or ends of phrases, and all the notes that fall on main beats. What I mean by the term "clean hand" is a stroke that is preceded by a stroke in the other hand. In other words, it is *not* the second note of a double sticking (as in LL or RR). When you have a "clean hand" available, you can play with a weighted stroke from your shoulder (mentioned earlier) and can better control the tone with which you play. To achieve this, I often use double-stickings just before the important note I want to play with the clean hand. (More will be said on this in Section III–B: Relationship of Sticking Choices to Phrasing.)

Sight-Reading

Being a good sight-reader is extremely useful. In certain jobs, it's critical to be able to sight-read. Good sight-readers generally learn music quickly. For many musicians it is a great comfort to feel confident about their sight-reading abilities.

Oftentimes, people who came to the marimba by way of studying the piano are excellent sight-readers. People who came to the marimba by way of drumset or other percussion often struggle with sight-reading. The reason for this is very simple: Pianists have had much more experience reading keyboard music. You may just need more experience.

That said, sight-reading can be a frustrating skill to practice. The reason is that we usually practice so that we will sound good. When you are practicing sight-reading, your primary goal should *not* be to sound good, but *to read every note on the page:* to make sense of what is written as quickly as possible and to realize it on the marimba. (If you happen to also sound good, it's a bonus!)

You can only sight-read something once. Of course, if you had difficulty reading something the first time, there will most likely be benefits to going over the material again, but realize that you are then not sight-reading.

There is no shortage of material to sight-read, and there never will be. Depending on your level, there is this entire book. If you are not up to this level yet, look for collections of single-line melodies for marimba or any treble or bass instrument. If you're taking college theory, play through your sight-singing book. Play the vocal line of any piano/vocal songbook from a show or album you like. Borrow books from your friends. When you're ready to get a little more adventurous, classical guitar music works well (as you can see from several adaptations included in Section IV). Then try easy piano music.

There are two basic approaches to practicing sight-reading.

Method 1: Select a piece, quickly survey it, and quickly choose a tempo on your metronome that you think you will be able to maintain throughout the piece. If in doubt, choose a slightly faster tempo that will push you a bit. Then, GO! You absolutely *must* stay with the metronome! If you get confused for a couple of beats (or even a couple of bars) and drop out of playing, keep your place in the music and jump back in as soon as you can.

The real-life application of this type of sight-reading practice is a situation in which you must sight-read with other people; they are not going to stop for you. You will be of most help to them, and most professional, if you don't call attention to your errors but just get back on track as quickly as possible.

Method 2: Decide on an approximate, conservative tempo, so that the rhythms you play will have some basis for making sense, but treat the tempo somewhat flexibly. Forget the metronome. Slow down a little when something is tricky so you can be relatively certain you got it right. Proceed at whatever pace is comfortable. You are not going to feel as "pushed" as with the first method.

The real-life application of this method is how you might approach a piece you have to learn for a rehearsal *tomorrow.* You'd want to get some sense of the tempo, but also not rush through the difficult things and learn them incorrectly. You need to really see what's there and, even though you can be somewhat relaxed, you know you have to work fairly efficiently.

Here are some general guidelines to always apply when sight-reading. When you initially survey a new piece you should, within a few seconds, notice:

1. the time signature
2. the tempo
3. stylistic markings (such as "rubato," "swung eighths," or mood directives such as "Cantabile")
4. the key signature
5. frequency of accidentals (extra flats, sharps, or naturals)
6. the dynamic landscape (Do the dynamics fluctuate a lot, or is there a section marked at one dynamic and another section at a contrasting dynamic?)
7. melodic contours (Are there scale patterns, recurring intervals, wide intervallic leaps, combinations of these?)
8. rhythmic variety (Are there recurring rhythms, or any challenging-looking rhythms that you should quickly unravel before starting?)

From this initial survey, you should feel confident about what lies ahead. You should also feel prepared to continually read ahead. For example, if the piece is relatively simple, in moderate 4/4 time, you should be able to take in two beats' worth, and as you're playing the first two beats, be reading the *next* two beats. In some cases, you could be reading a bar or two ahead of what you're playing. In some cases, you will only be able to read a beat ahead but, to sight-read well, you *must* be looking ahead!

Sight-reading is significantly easier if you can minimize how much you need to look down at the keyboard. (See Section I-H. Learning the Keyboard Layout.) As you practice sight-reading, make a concerted effort to keep your eyes on the music as much as possible.

How to Practice

Regular practice is essential to improving and should be a process that is both enjoyable and productive. Here are some guidelines that may help.

Schedule time to practice on a regular basis. You may want to do this at the time of day you feel you can concentrate best. If you don't always have the luxury of being able to practice at that time, the most important thing is that you develop the discipline to *do it,* whenever it *is* possible. You may find it's helpful to look ahead and block out practice times in your schedule. Try to adhere to these as responsibly as you would other appointments.

It should go without saying but if, for some reason, you experience any kind of physical discomforts or pain as you play, do *not* continue to practice just to meet your time quota! Everyone has certain physical limits.

It can be enjoyable to work on several different things during your practice sessions. For instance, in any given practice session you might practice:

1. a primary solo you are learning
2. a contrasting solo that might be at a more beginning stage
3. sight-reading (both for the experience of sight-reading, and as a means of scoping out new repertoire possibilities)
4. rudimentary skills (such as the rhythmic exercises in Section I–I. Basics of Good Rhythm and "Feel" or various items from Section I-F. Scales)
5. difficult passages from music you're learning

I often use the latter as a warm-up. In each practice session, I recommend you have a notepad handy to make a list of passages you find most challenging in whatever music you are learning (for example, "mm. 40–47"). A short list of these is great to tackle at the beginning of a practice session as a warm-up.

When most people begin to practice, they are a little "spaced out"—perhaps still thinking about the last thing they were doing, or something that happened earlier in the day. When I'm in this transitional state of mind at the beginning of a practice session, it's very useful to slowly go over the most difficult passages of the music I'm currently working on (which I listed in the previous practice session). Sometimes I expand on elements in the music (by repeating short, difficult sections) and create little exercises using the difficult material I need to get in my hands. Then, when I come across them later while playing the complete piece, they will be a little more familiar. "Rudimentary skills" also make good warm-ups/transitions into more concentrated work.

Some guidelines on practicing solos:

1. Don't always start at the beginning! Many people make that mistake, and never spend enough time on later sections of the music.
2. *Especially* don't start at the beginning, play until you get "stuck," and return to the beginning! You will keep getting stuck in the same place! If this happens, really study the place you get stuck, and figure out why you do. Then start just before that spot and practice getting through the difficult passage. Practice it *a lot* before you try going back to the beginning to see how you fare with it in the larger context.
3. Practice a new piece slowly; it's important to really digest what's there and not learn something incorrectly. However, don't *only* practice slowly. I think it's extremely useful, when you're learning something, to also jump into playing it at tempo—even if you can only do so for a beat at a time. It shows you what you need to work toward, and how fast your hands will be moving. It's also a good "reality check" on whether your stickings will work when you get up to the real tempo. Come at learning a piece from two directions: slowly, *and* little bits up to tempo.
4. It's very helpful to play one line or phrase many times repeatedly. Some people get nervous that they'll never get through a piece if they spend too much time on one section. But, actually, it's tremendously efficient in the long run. When you play one phrase many times consecutively, you will start to discover much deeper things about it, both in terms of subtle technical challenges that exist and how to overcome them, and underlying features of the music which you might wish to expand on.
5. Break long lines into smaller sections so they're not so overwhelming. Even as you perform, sometimes group fast lines in your mind by each beat. For example, visualize a long stretch of sixteenth notes in groups of four (beamed) notes.
6. Try what I call "the tempo game." The "game" is that you start to play a piece and have license to play at absolutely any tempo you want—except you cannot play any note unless you are *absolutely certain* you will not make a mistake. So, if a piece is easy at the beginning, you could start at tempo and then, when it gets trickier, slow down (suddenly is okay!) to any tempo at which you are sure you can play the music perfectly. This is great for practicing staying focused and increasing your concentration, not to mention improving your note accuracy.
7. Don't hesitate to make notes to yourself in your music. It's probably best to only write the minimum needed to be a reminder; you don't want the page to be too cluttered. (I'm not a fan of keeping individual pages of music in plastic sleeves. It's fine for your master copy of a piece but, when you're working on a piece, I think it's nice to be able to more freely touch the music and make it yours.)

It's natural that the progress you make one day will have partly slipped away when you start to practice the next day. It might feel like you take two steps forward and one step back. But, you can at least feel confident that the first step, or bit of ground you maintained, is pretty firmly ingrained in your mind and hands. This phenomenon is one reason that consistent practicing is so important. In fact, frequent practice is more important than "spaced out" long sessions. Don't hesitate to take short breaks to keep your mind fresh.

It's really important to learn a lot of music. While it's beneficial to learn some pieces thoroughly in order to perform them, I think it's a mistake to stay on one piece too long until it's absolutely perfect; you'll get bored. This is one reason I recommend always having at least one contrasting piece—or *something* else you're working on—besides one main solo. Musicians grow the most by playing a lot of music.

If you find you can memorize music easily, I encourage you to play some pieces by memory. But be very careful that you have learned them correctly. If you memorize something incorrectly, it can be very difficult to relearn it. With pieces you have learned very well and memorized, I recommend returning to the written music occasionally just to make sure you have not begun to distort anything.

Section Two 50 Short Four-Mallet Studies

Composed by Nancy Zeltsman

These short studies demonstrate various techniques of four-mallet marimba playing, many of which will be applicable to other music. There is a sort of "game" behind each one; in some cases, a few techniques are showcased within a single study. Most are not "technical" exercises in the traditional sense of providing a "work-out" for your hands; they are meant to be more mentally and musically challenging. Many of the studies are a bit quirky and unpredictable—to keep you on your toes!

It is important that you adhere to every sticking indicated (at least if you want to get the full effect of what I meant for each study to reveal). As a reminder, stickings are numbered left to right, with 1 being the bass mallet and 4 being the soprano mallet. In many cases, stickings that apply to the right hand (mallets 3 and 4) are written above the staff (or on the top staff), and stickings pertaining to the left hand (mallets 1 and 2) are written below the staff (or on the bottom staff). When a sticking is followed by an arrow, it means to continue using that mallet until further notice. When there are two stickings with arrows, along with (alt.), it means to alternate the two stickings with arrows until further notice.

The studies are purposefully short to emphasize the virtues of playing a short segment of music repeatedly until you truly understand it and have mastered it. Also, for intermediate and advanced players who would benefit from sight-reading these studies, I hope their shortness will make them more inviting and approachable. (In my experience, longer pieces can be daunting to those who need to practice sight-reading.)

Accidentals hold through the bar (as in traditional notation). When a range of metronome marks is given, it means you can select any number within that range. (By the way, many of the studies could also be played on a vibraphone, although some will need to be transposed up one octave.)

Generally, these studies are not intended as concert pieces (studies 41, 47 and 49 are possible exceptions). However, they could certainly be performed in educational settings. Also, if a player wishes to devise and perform a suite of six to ten studies of his or her choice, I would not object.

These were fun to write! I encourage players who enjoy them to compose similar studies themselves, and to continually add to their collection.

1

In this study, based on the interval of a tritone, each mallet plays only one note. This enables you to focus on triggering each mallet with a clear, directed stroke. The 5/4 time signature is intended to pose a bit of a challenge (if most of your experience has been with 4/4 time).

2

You begin with each mallet corresponding to only one note, but in m. 3 the inner mallets change notes; then the outer mallets change notes in m. 4. In m. 5 you reset to the opening notes. In m. 7 the note changes occur more quickly. Try to visualize the note shifts a couple of beats, or an entire bar, ahead of time. Try to make the notes in m. 1 and m. 5 have a "horizontal" phrased feel, in contrast to the other patterns, which are more "vertical" and static.

3

Within a moderate tempo such as this, long lines can sound smoothest when played with the same mallet. The recommended stickings set up a comfortable shift between the first and second line of the piece, and between the last two notes. Try to use center beating spots on the "black notes" if you can get to them gracefully; otherwise, using the edge beating spots is fine.

4

As a reminder, sticking indication such as "2–>", "3–>" and "alt." designate that you alternate between mallets 2 and 3. This study provides examples of playing mainly with two mallets and occasionally integrating another mallet to facilitate a wide interval skip (for example, the reach up to the high E in m. 4) to keep your overall motion to a minimum.

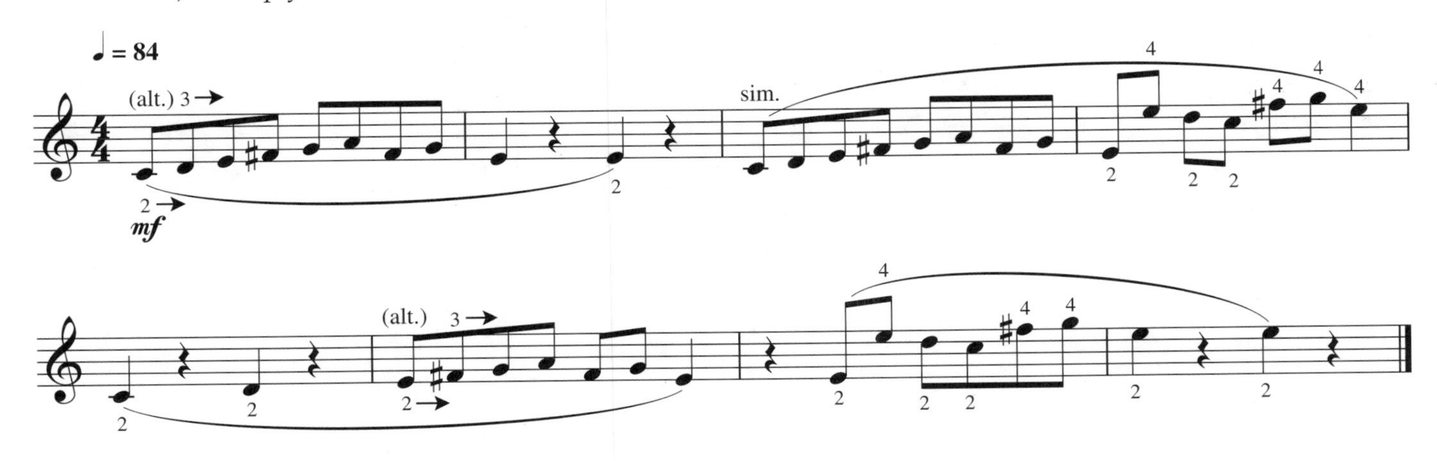

5

This study is a play on "all black notes" vs. "all white notes" (except for a surprise in the last measure). It provides excellent opportunities for preparing your mallets to play—that is, getting them in place, hovering over the bars—*before* you need to play. For example, near the end of m. 2, your left hand can already be moving to where it needs to be in order to play m. 3, and your right hand can join it and *be in place* to play m. 3 before you need to play. Similarly you can prepare ahead to play m. 3, beat 4, and so on.

6

This study focuses on hand independence as well as coordination. Your left hand sets up a waltz feel and can then go on "automatic pilot"; the right hand plays different material on top. In association with practicing this study, you could try a little improvisation. Play the left-hand pattern as written but, with the right hand, play *any* A-flats and D-flats, together or separately, in any rhythm.

7

Here, the phrases emphasize the harmonic progression. Try to play with a legato, sweeping feeling across each phrase. To accomplish this, take care with the relative dynamics from note to note. Strive for a subtle *diminuendo* across each phrase. No notes should pop out suddenly. Note the unusual voicing of the last chord; it will sound more consonant if you emphasize the C (by pressing a little harder with mallet 3).

8

This provides an opportunity to work on the dynamic balance between your hands (the right hand accompanies the left). Try to bring out the tenutos, the different phrase lengths, and slight dynamic changes. In the last few bars, use the time you have in the rests to prepare the final chords.

9

This one, based on a G-flat major scale, is intentionally a little unusual to count. (Count in half notes.) The character of the piece is stately, refined and poised. The last bar should sound very smooth. Enjoy pacing the fade-out.

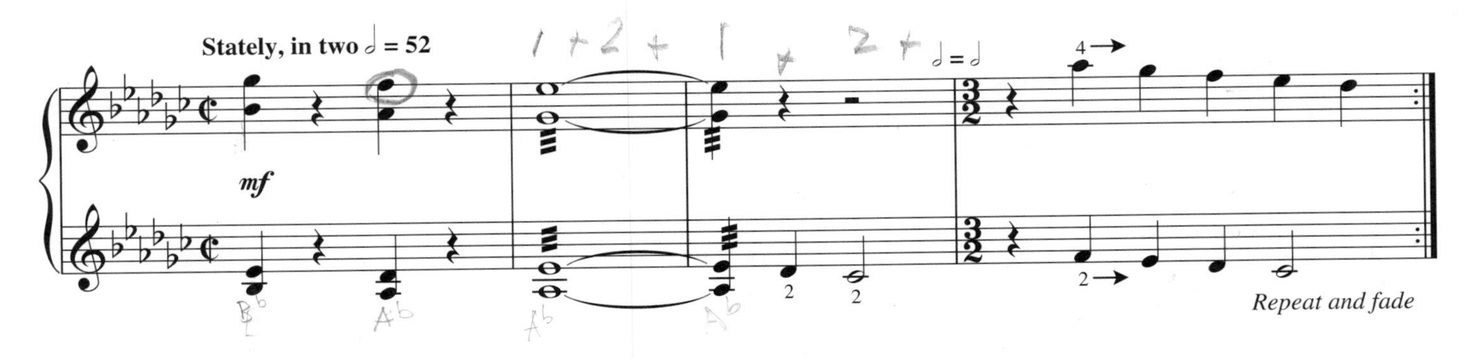

10

This introduces a typical four-mallet configuration of notes: mallets 1, 2, 3, 4—combined with a few surprises. At the end, the four notes of each rolled chord should initially be struck together (as opposed to the two notes of one hand, followed by the two notes in the other hand).

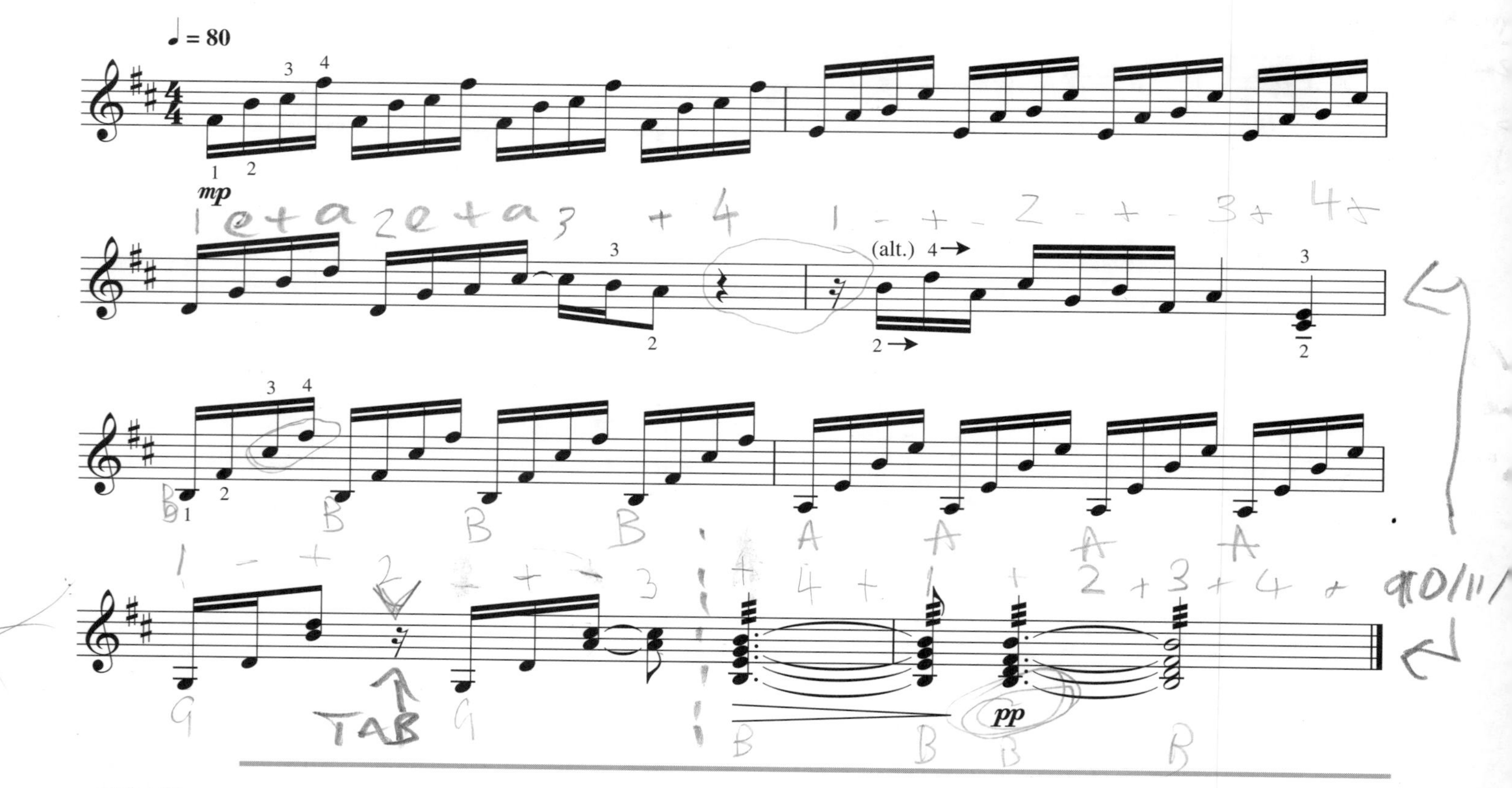

11

This study centers on intervals of a third, not only between the two mallets of each hand, but between your two inner mallets. Note that the "2 feel" of the 6/8 is interrupted in m. 2 and m. 6 due to the placement of accents in those bars, which results in their having a 3/4 feel. There are also opportunities to practice intervals of a second. The somewhat unusual articulations marked in m. 4 and in the last bar (staccato, accent, *and* "ring" mark) are meant to suggest a "pingy" attack (which might best be achieved by a rather quick downstroke and upstroke), followed by a bell-like ring.

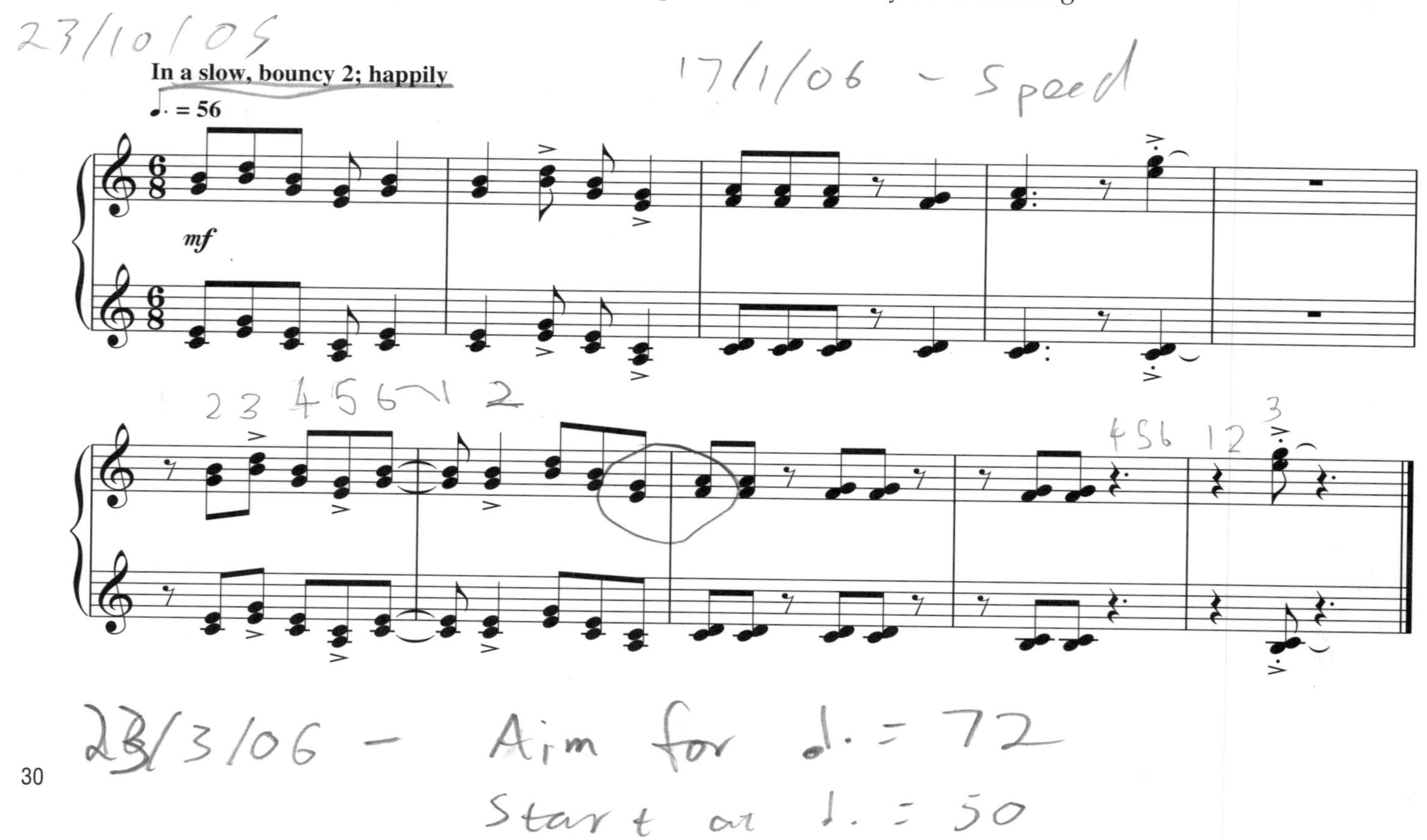

12

Roll all notes and try to create a smooth texture. When a chord enters at the beginning of a phrase, try to have all four notes enter together (whereas, *within* a series of chords, it matters less if two notes of a chord enter slightly before the other two notes). In the last three bars, you are given the somewhat unusual task of bringing out the alto voice.

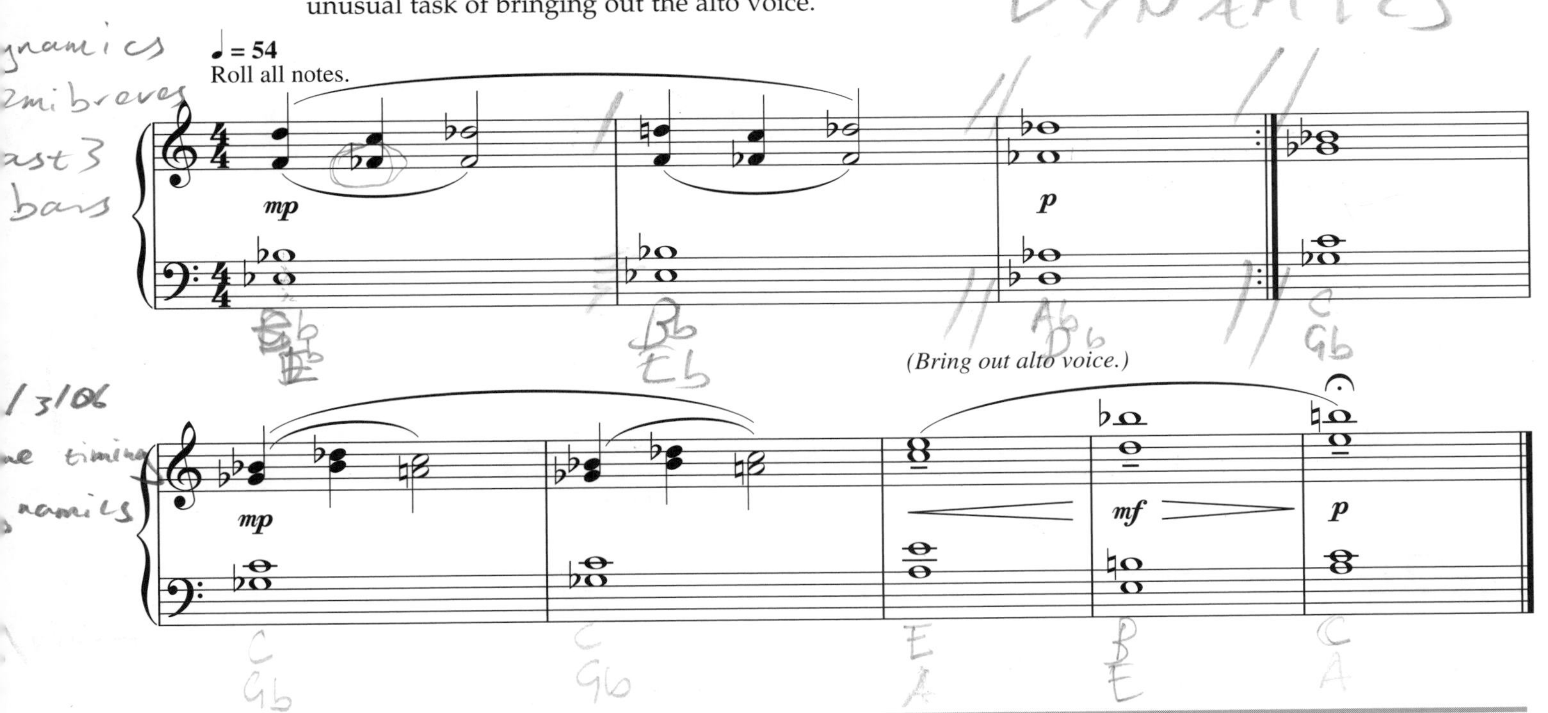

13

Some people find it difficult to keep time while playing rolls, since it often means doing something precise (counting) at the same time you are doing something free (rolling at no particular speed relative to the tempo). In this study, you could opt to play measured rolls (a predetermined number of alternations per beat) to help keep your place. However, it is also fine to play unmeasured rolls here. The final chords provide an opportunity to practice dead strokes.

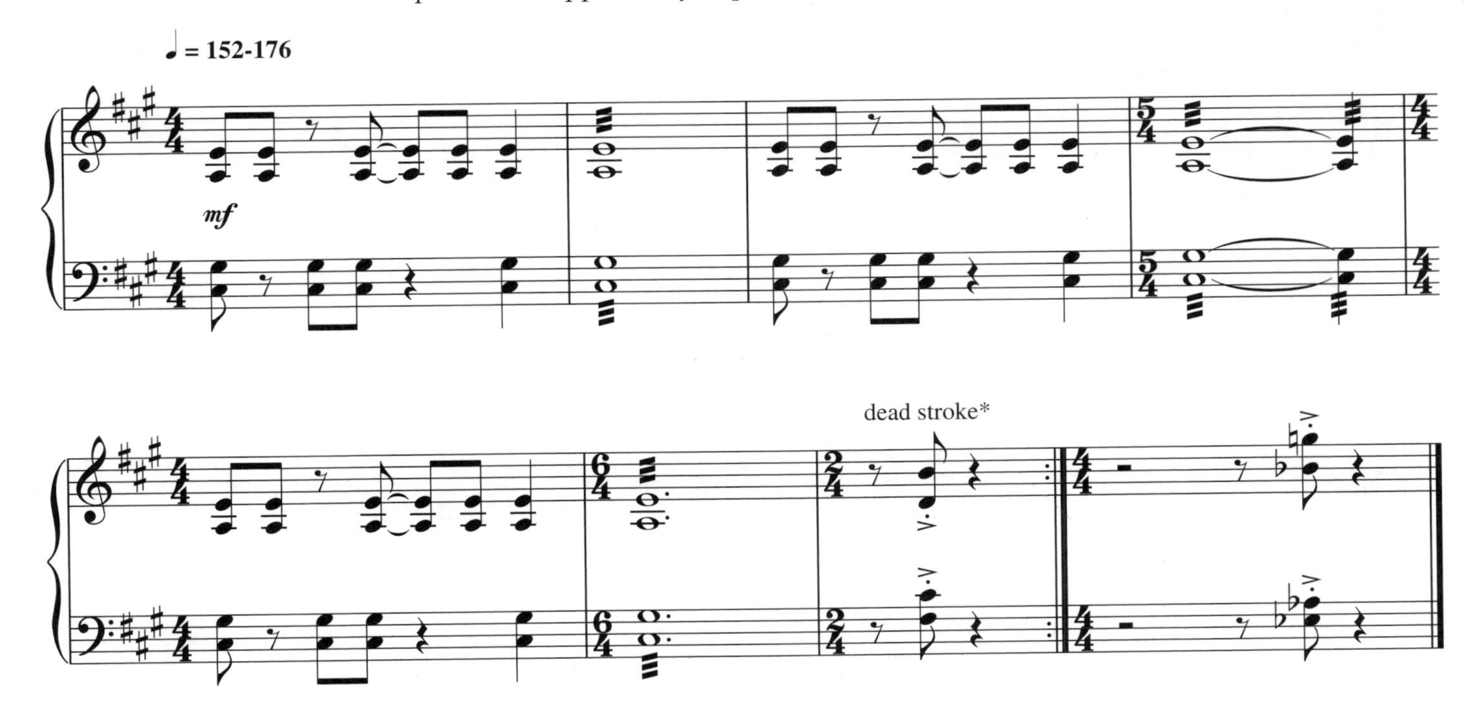

*Choke the sound by pressing mallet heads into bars.

14

Each successive chord, containing the identical inner intervalic relationship, moves only a half step (up or down) from the previous chord. Because of this, the study introduces very typical moves of mallet players: frequent shifts between different combinations of "white" and "black" notes. Be thoughtful about choosing good beating spots. At a dynamic of ***p***, using the edge beating spots of the "black" notes will sound fine. This will also keep your movements to a minimum and give a smooth look to your playing. Do use center beating spots when they are easy to reach. Subtle repositionings of your body (which enable less contortion of your wrists and arms) can often help to support these shifts. Roll only where indicated.

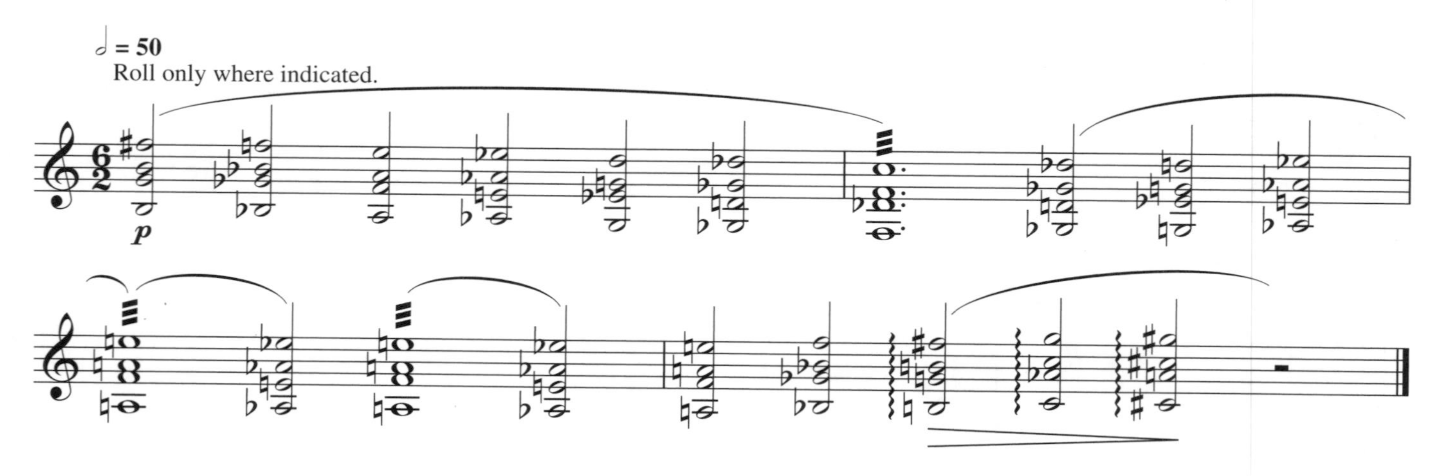

15

This study provides a chance to practice playing intervals of fourths, fifths, and sixths and changing between them.

16

When first learning one-handed rolls, it can be very helpful to sometimes play a roll with two hands, and then try to copy the sound of that (competent) roll with one hand. (Having the "ideal" sound in mind can sometimes work miracles!) Following the directions given, you will alternate between playing these rolls with two hands and playing them with one hand. (Play the one-handed roll in the last bar with mallet 1 on the center beating spot, and mallet 2 on the edge beating spot. To do this, shift your weight [and maybe also take a step] to the left and play with your left elbow out, supporting the aforementioned position of the mallets.)

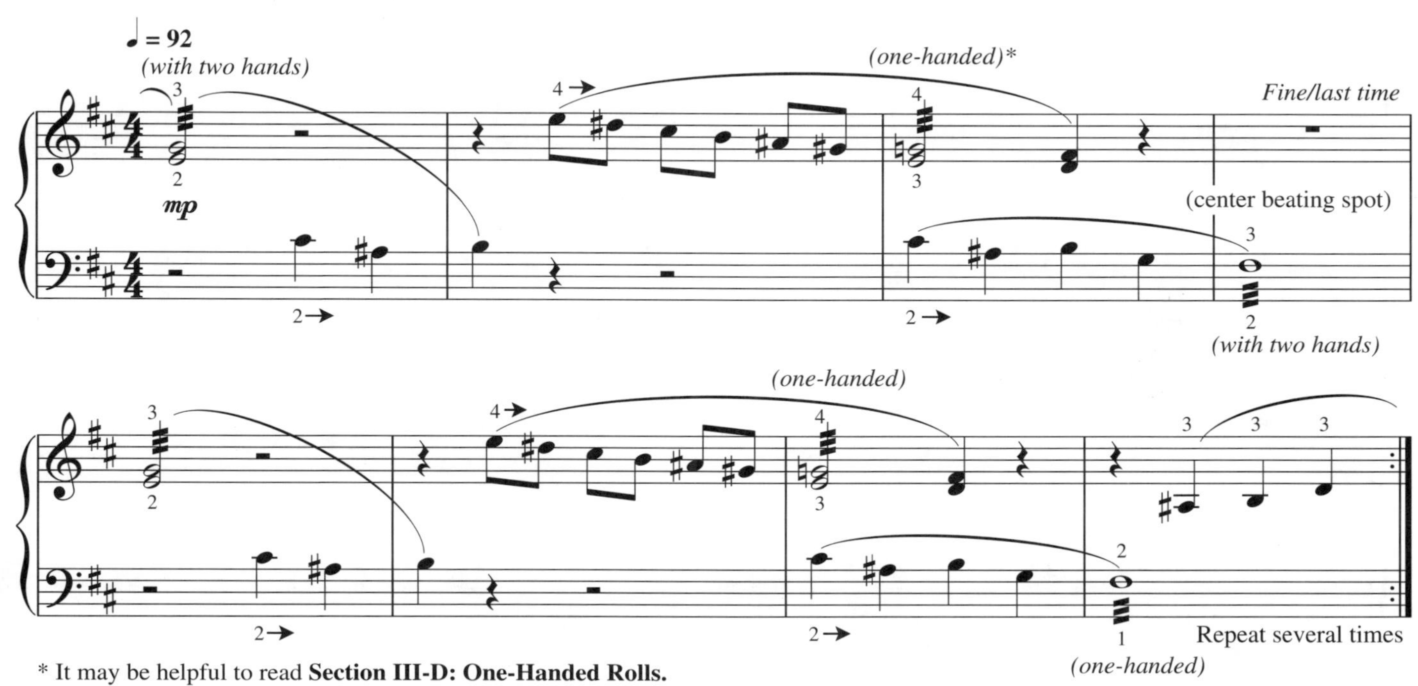

* It may be helpful to read **Section III-D: One-Handed Rolls.**

15/12/05

17

Try to play each phrase smoothly. The stickings center on alternations between the inner mallets, but include some double-stickings that flatter the phrasing (and keep higher notes played by the right hand, and lower notes played by the left hand). The outer mallets are used occasionally to assist with big reaches.

tap foot

18

This study introduces good stickings for upward arpeggios. Try to play them gracefully, taking care with the relative dynamics of notes within each group; no note should stick out, and each group should have a nice dynamic shape relative to the next group within the *diminuendo* or *crescendo*. In m. 3, try to shift smoothly from the one-handed roll into a roll alternating between hands for the last two beats.

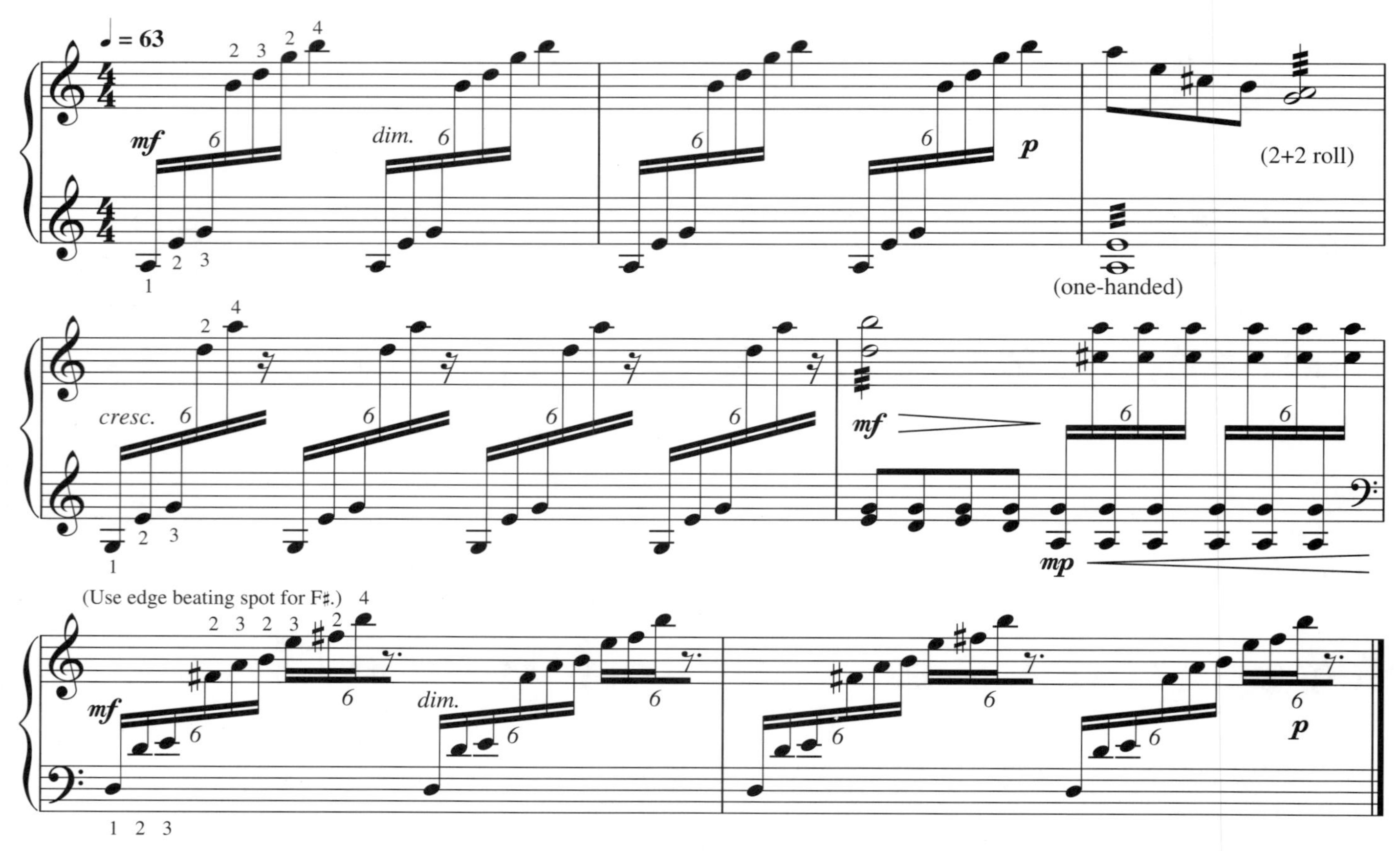

19

Roll all notes. The suggested stickings enable smooth transitions between rolls. It may be helpful to read Section III-C. Refining Rolls, Legato Rolls.

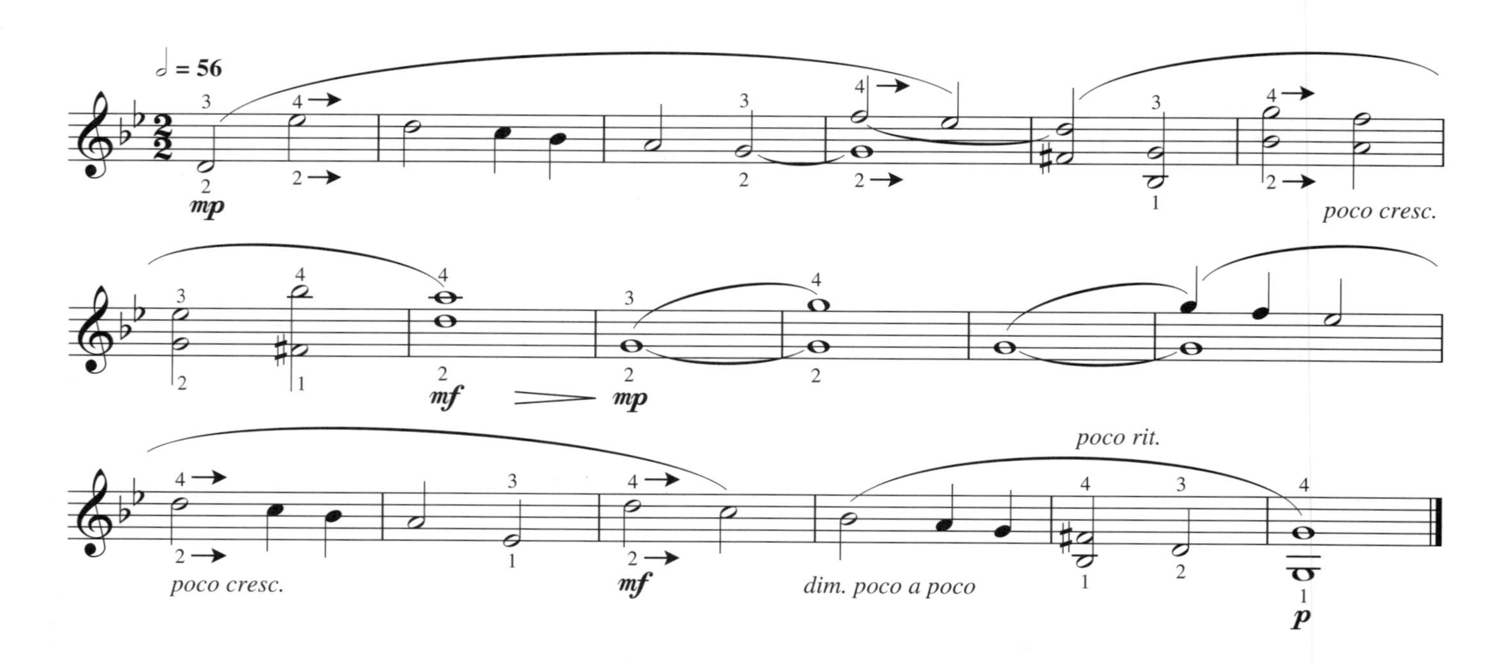

20

This presents some typical configurations of four-mallet playing. mm. 1–4 employ the same configuration I use for a "ripple" roll (mallets 1, 2, 4, 3), but here it is slowed down; at a dynamic of f, you must play with very clearly-directed strokes. The accents played by mallet 2 in mm. 3–4 may present a challenge. When the note configuration changes in mm. 5–6 to one that lies more comfortably, be careful not to rush; maintain good control of even sixteenth notes.

21

Focus on playing smooth, long lines with tenuto strokes. Two-against-three rhythms are introduced, as well as triple to duple shifts of feel.

22

This study focuses on playing with full "tenuto" strokes (where marked). It also presents some coordination challenges. Be thoughtful about the dynamic balance between hands; sometimes the ostinato is featured. Try to play long, smooth phrases. The study also offers the opportunity to practice shifts between intervals of a sixth up to a ninth.

23

Gently pulse each dotted-quarter beat. This offers a slightly tricky note pattern as well as the need to target and accent notes located in outer extremes in either direction (in homage to Jacob Druckman's "Reflections on the Nature of Water," second movement).

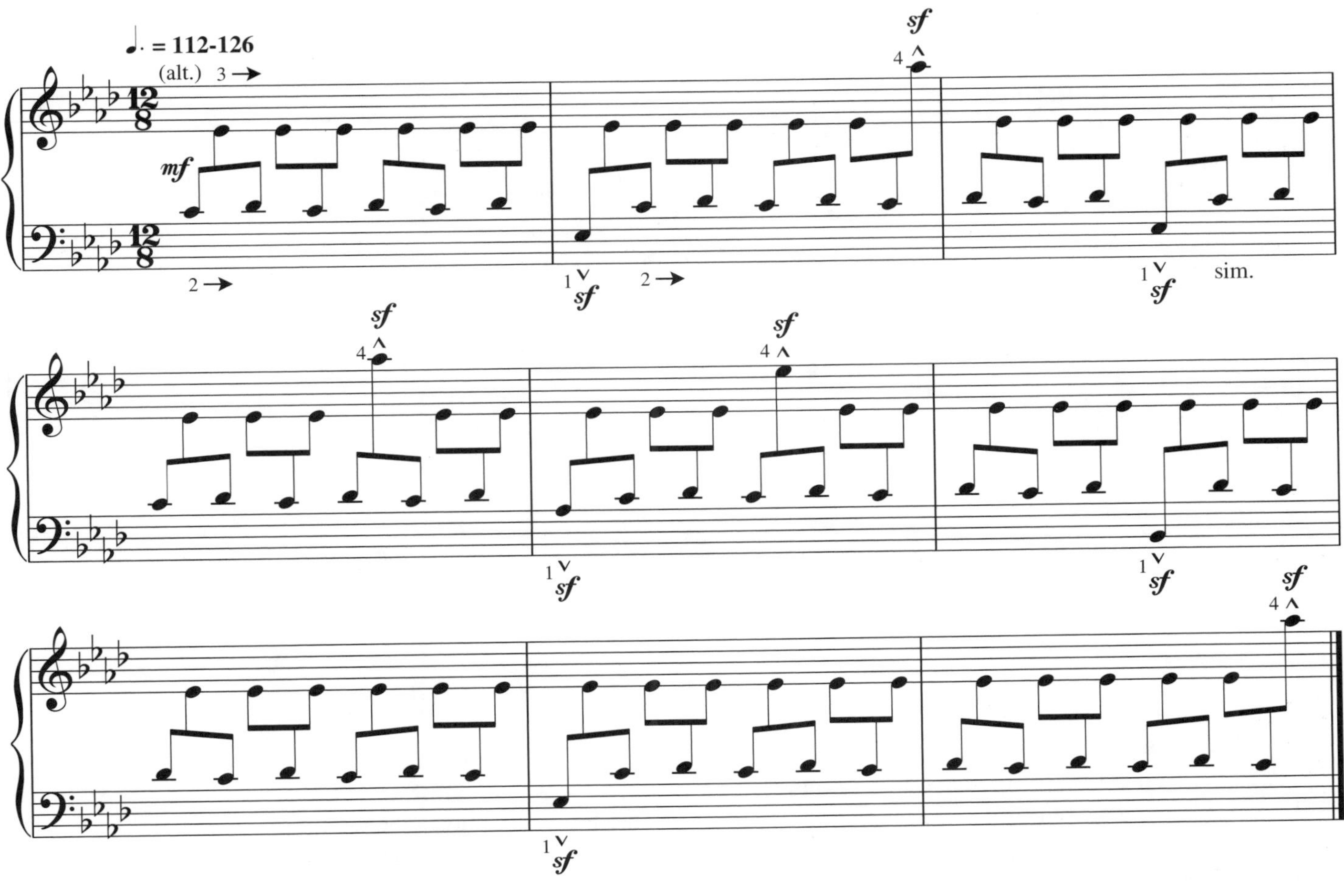

24

Roll all notes. Consider which notes to bring out in order to clearly project the phrases and harmonic movement.

25

Roll all notes except sixteenth notes. It can be difficult to play smooth rolls on lines that move quickly, especially at a full dynamic; your rolls will need to be rather fast. This study offers stickings that, by reducing motion, should aid in smoother shifts. It also presents the challenge of controlling fast hand alternations but switching which mallet within one hand is playing. Always redistribute your body weight into supportive positions from which to play the chords *before* you need to play them.

26

Various stickings, including double-stickings, are specified to minimize movement and enhance phrasing. Emphasize the moods created through the various phrase lengths. mm. 1, 2 and 6 should have a lilting feel; m. 3 should feel long and legato; mm. 4 and 5 should have a smooth, suspended feeling due to the slow two-against-three rhythm (also seen in the first half of m. 3).

27

This study gets your hands moving in even alternations. Despite your hands' constant motion, prepare for each shift in interval size before you need to make it.

28

Roll all notes. In this fairly high register of the marimba, it is more difficult to make rolls sound smooth than it is in the lower registers. It helps to roll quite fast. Personally, I feel that fast ripple rolls have a wonderful "sparkling" quality in this range.

29

This study focuses on larger intervals, particularly octaves. The main challenges are bringing out the phrases and subtle dynamic shifts.

30

Stand with your hip against the D and E to deaden them. Despite standing in this unusual position, try to play the ostinato steadily and confidently. Bars with repeat signs should only be repeated once. The rhythms in the right hand may be a little challenging to coordinate. Overall, this provides a good drill of shifts between duple and triple subdivisions. Always look/think ahead!

31

Roll all notes. Emphasize each pitch marked with a tenuto until the next one. It may be helpful to read Section III-C. Refining Rolls, Balancing Chords.

32

In the middle and upper registers of the marimba, it is not uncommon for mallet players (especially jazz players) to use mallets 2 and 4. Why not practice the opposite: mallets 1 and 3 (applied in the lower registers)? In the course of this study, many different sticking combinations are used. My goal was to introduce some unusual, but plausible stickings (which use minimal movements). Note that m. 6 marks a sudden dynamic contrast; it should seem like a sudden echo, or rhythmic underpinning, until melodic material returns in m. 7, beat 2. (The underpinning material returns in m. 8.)

33

This obviously centers around the sticking configuration 4, 3, 1, 2. It can be challenging to articulate quickly changing patterns in close intervals (such as fourths). Try to clearly articulate all notes.

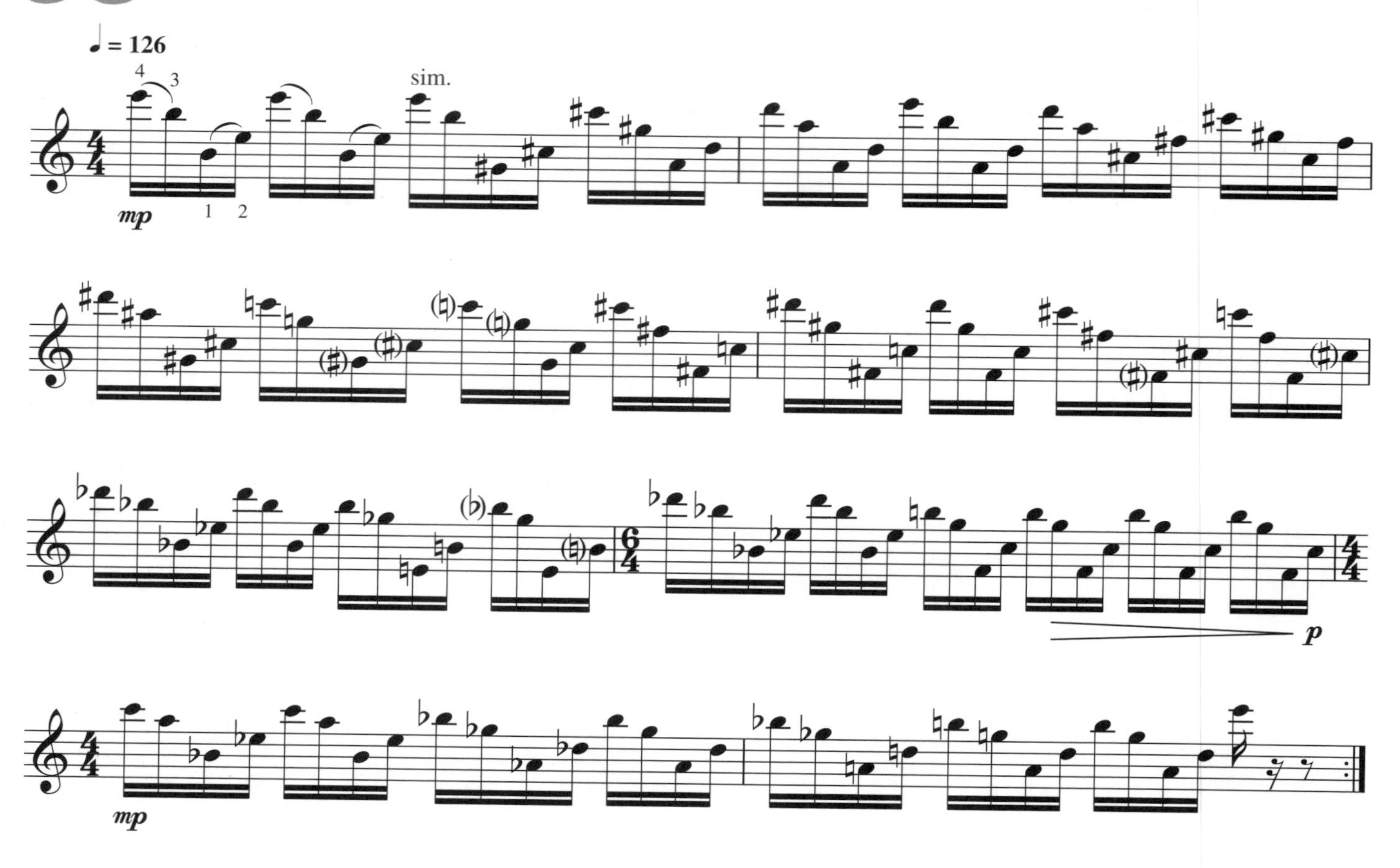

34

The focus here is one-handed rolls and dynamic control of them.

35

Try to play with a full (rather than harsh) tone. It is quite challenging to play the intervals of a second interspersed with larger intervals. Try to shift to the various-sized intervals *before* you need to play them.

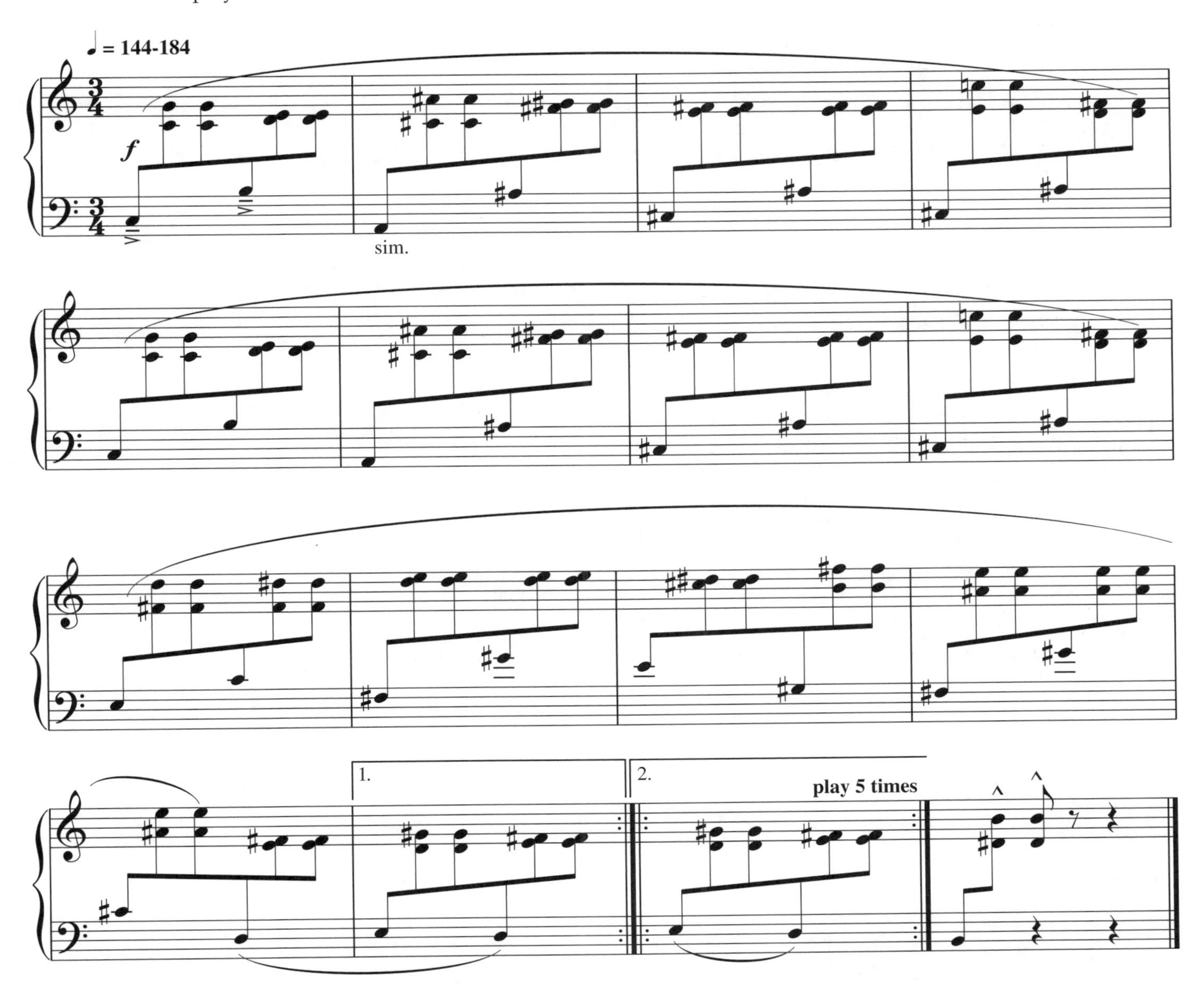

36

All double-stops should attack together (*then* be rolled). It can be quite tricky to play these alternating, slightly overlapping, *forte* one-handed rolls.

37

Focus on establishing a nice, relaxed groove. On top of this, try to project the subtle dynamic changes/balances and phrases.

38

Try counting out loud or tonguing quarter and eighth notes while you play this one. Grace notes are to be played *on* the beat.

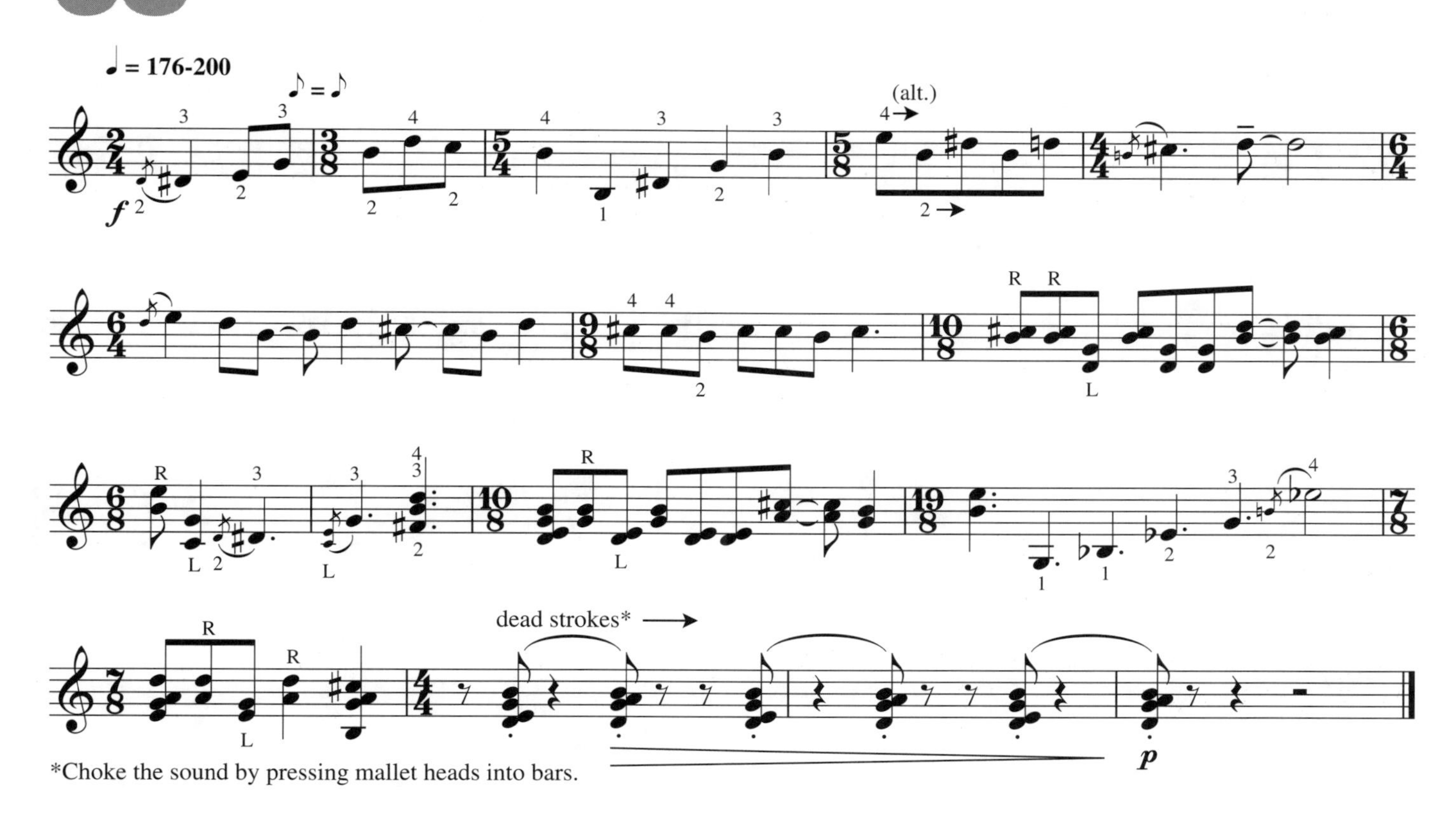

*Choke the sound by pressing mallet heads into bars.

39

For Jack Van Geem The beaming is intended to suggest playing this piece as one very smooth, long line. The idea behind the stickings (which are somewhat unusual) is keeping movements to a minimum. Try keeping your mallets extremely low to the keyboard and make very quick, smooth shifts.

40

Rhythmic accuracy will be aided by tonguing/subdividing in sixteenth notes. You might also record clicks or claps (or have a friend play these with you) in eighth notes and dotted-eighth notes—a challenging study in itself!—and play with this.

41

For Keiko Kotoku This lyrical study focuses on playing short phrases. To accomplish this effect, refer to the "hairpin *diminuendo*" idea introduced in Section I-J. Basics of Good Phrasing. Of course, there should also be a sense of the long phrase (across all the little ones).

42

This study has several challenging elements. It is important to clearly differentiate between duple and triple rhythms. Some of the triple-rhythms have a "swung" feel, but the eighth-note-based rhythms should not feel swung. There are also many quick shifts between chords, different kinds of articulations to strive for, ***fp*** chord entrances, phrases across quarter-note triplets, one-handed rolls with *crescendi*, and the need to come off rolls and immediately land on a chord.

43

The trills in this study, which all begin on the upper note, must be very fast and timed so that they end exactly on the following beat. There are also other ornamental figures in which fast notes must be played very precisely. These stickings provide some ideas of how you can use four mallets to assist you in playing passages that, at first glance, seem like two-mallet material.

44

For Ray Dillard This study centers on the same issues as Study 43; however, it covers a broader range of the instrument. Note that, from the fourth beat of m. 2 through m. 3, the phrases suggest the feeling of four 5/16 bars (superimposed over the 4/4 pulse). Despite all the activity in the piece, it is important to keep a steady pulse throughout, and to carefully place the last note exactly in time.

45

For Ron Samuels This is a study in lyrical, thoughtfully-balanced playing using many one-handed rolls.

*This is an unusual situation in which it may work best to have your left arm and mallets from an "L" configuration, and play the one-handed roll with an almost "up/down" wrist movement (as opposed to a sideways rotation).

46

For Steve Mackey All grace notes are to be played ahead of the note written (as is traditional). This presents some unusual configurations of notes as well as an opportunity to practice quintuplets.

47

For Bogdan Bácanu The phrasing and tempo shifts in this piece should be approached very playfully in order to project a lyrical, sweet, and sometimes cute, sentiment. Trills begin on the upper note.

48

Different-speed rolls are specified here, which create a particular atmosphere in particular registers of the marimba. Try to imply a nice, lilting flow of the 9/8 pulse (three beats per bar). At the end, there is an unusual request for a "black-note" gliss with mallet 2, closely trailed by mallet 4. You must gliss very quickly and lightly in order not to get stuck in the cracks.

49

For Fumito Nunoya This piece delves into two-against-three rhythms. Try to play the ***f***s and ***ff***s with a big, full sound (as opposed to a harsh one). The study also presents chords with unusual arm positions (for example, m. 4, last dotted-eighth), and various articulations including accents/staccatos, tenutos, and dead strokes.

50

For Nanae Mimura Roll all notes. Try to play very lyrically with smooth rolls and clear phrases, emphasizing the notes marked with tenutos. The quarter notes should help to keep a sense of forward momentum. The connection of the first line into the second line of music poses an interesting challenge; be creative with the types of rolls you choose to use. For instance, you could play the F-sharp/A-sharp at the end of m. 2 as a one-handed roll and maintain that while playing the left hand in m. 3 as quick, repeated double-stops. (The dynamic is soft enough that this technique will probably blend fine and sound smooth.) Or, you could try to slip smoothly from that one-handed roll (in the right hand) into a "2+2" (alternated-hands) roll at the beginning of m. 3.

Repeat as many times as desired.

3A Refining Strokes and Tone Production

In Section I-D. Basic Strokes and Tone Production, I described my basic stroke. Hopefully, you've experimented with various types of strokes and discovered certain basic arm/wrist motions that both sound good and feel natural to you: *your* personal basic stroke. Here are some specifics about how you can sometimes vary your basic stroke and tone in order to make your playing more colorful and expressive.

Articulations

This is by no means a complete list of possibilities. Subtle shifts of finger pressure and various types and combinations of down/upstrokes, stroke speed, wrist, and arm movements can produce numerous different articulations and musical nuances in your playing—some quite difficult to describe, yet very colorful and effective in evoking different musical attitudes.

Staccatos: When notes are marked staccato, I sometimes play them as dead strokes (completely dampening the note with the mallet head as it is struck) or quasi-dead-strokes (dampening, but not pressing as hard, so the resonance isn't quite as choked). Another way I make a note sound short is to approach it with a very quick downstroke and upstroke. The result is a light, airy sound that is effective if you want the note to be short but ring a little.

Accents: My goal is that accented notes not just seem slightly louder relative to the notes around them, but that they have a distinctly sharp attack. To achieve this, I use a very fast downstroke combined with some wrist snap. (I don't think so much about the upstroke; it's mainly just a rebound from the wrist snap.)

The difficult thing here is timing. Relative to a normal-speed stroke on an unaccented note, you need to compensate for how quickly the fast, snappy stroke will arrive. I suggest practicing rather slow, repeated strokes on one note, played by one hand at a time, maintaining a dynamic level of ***mf***. Play a series of normal strokes and then accented strokes, and also alternate between them, making sure that your tempo remains absolutely steady

when you play the accents. Then try this at other dynamic levels. Ultimately, you should be able to play, for instance, an accented ***mp*** note and have it sound distinctly different from a normal ***mf*** note, and be able to make such differences between any adjacent dynamic levels.

Tenutos: These require a very slow downstroke and sluggish, small upstroke. They are only a slight variation to my basic stroke, which I described for achieving a full tone in I-D. Basic Strokes and Tone Production. I try to "caress" the bars with the mallet, almost as if the mallet head has a strong magnetic attraction to the bar.

Staccato/tenuto: Do a medium-fast downstroke that afterwards remains almost on the bar for a split-second, followed by a deliberate upstroke.

Accent/tenuto: Do a fast downstroke with wrist-snap which, after the point of contact, gets kind of "stuck": that is, almost no upstroke.

Sforzandi: Do a fast stroke with more attention to wrist snap, in order to make the sound more aggressive than a regular accent.

Timbre Shifts/Beating Spots

My personal favorite beating spots (described in I-C. Basic Beating Spots) are not universally endorsed. Instead of playing in the center of the bar over the resonator, many people prefer the timbre (that is, tone quality) available just off-center (lined up with the edge of the resonator, if you were looking straight down toward the resonator, or even at the spot that is equidistant between the center and the node). The off-center spots (on either side of the resonator tube) have a clearer fundamental pitch than does the center of the bar (over the resonator). The sound is a bit drier and matches the timbre of the edges of the bars quite well. Therefore, people think that the combination of playing off-center on the "white keys" and the edges of the "black keys" yields optimum uniformity of tone.

The tone at the center of the bars, however, is more full and resonant with a somewhat complicated assortment of harmonics included with the fundamental pitch. Personally, I like that more complicated richness, especially in the range from the C below middle-C to two octaves above middle-C. For me, the rich sound at the center of the bars is central to my general sound. It is minimally affected by the fact that I also use the edges of the "black keys" in faster passages in which I can't gracefully reach the centers (particularly at softer dynamics). In faster passages, the resonance of each note is not so noticeable anyway. Also, the top corner (that is, the very edge) of the "black notes" (which I try to strike at a diagonal) are actually quite "ringy" compared with playing on the tops of the ends of the bars a little ways from the node. In the top octave or so, you pretty much *have* to play in the center or you'll be too near the nodes.

In the lowest octave of a five-octave instrument I prefer to play off-center (either side of the resonator tube); this is the one exception to my preference for the centers. The reason is that, when it comes to playing bass notes, I want the fundamental pitch to be as clear as possible, even if I am sacrificing a little resonance. It's important for the bass pitches to be very clear, as they are the foundation of all the harmonies built above them.

Despite the fact that you generally want to avoid the nodes, for certain effects you can intentionally play on or near the node. This would work well when trying to emulate guitar harmonics, or if you want a particularly "pingy" or distant sound.

Some players don't make a choice between generally playing in the center of the bars or off-center. Instead, they intentionally and carefully make use of *all* the aforementioned beating spots in various circumstances and, therefore, consider the whole gamut as central to their basic sound.

Mallet Angling

To play softly (and distantly) in passages involving very little movement, one fairly common practice is tilting up the mallet handles so that the playing surface of the mallet becomes the fluffier part of the yarn, above the normal playing surface. (The less-often-used yarn sounds softer.) A typical application would be fading-in from (or fading-out to) "niente" (nothing, in terms of dynamics) on a roll. It is often combined with shifts in beating spots. For example, you could begin on the nodes to fade in a roll with angled mallets (that is, playing with the fluffier yarn). Then, as the roll *crescendos*, gradually move to richer-sounding beating spots and lower the mallet handles in order to return to the normal playing surface of the mallets. This creates a sense of the sound coming from very far away and gradually gaining more volume and presence—or vice versa.

It can certainly provide a poetic effect; however, I am always wary when I see people do it, and I virtually never do it myself. My concern is that players get so caught up in the fancy shifts they're making that they cease to listen to the sound they're making. I like my playing "voice" to remain fairly consistent. For *crescendos/diminuendos*, I use the normal playing surface of the mallet and my preferred beating spots, and focus on my tone as it relates to the increasing/decreasing presence of the sound.

Various Note Durations

It is a myth (at least, I *want* it to be!) that marimbists are not capable of playing different note durations. Many people, faced with having to play a sixteenth, eighth, quarter, half, or whole note would play it exactly the same way. They don't believe it's possible on marimba to do anything more than strike a note.

I remember being told as a young piano student not to lift my fingers off the keys on the final chord of a piece, even if the pedal was accomplishing the required sustain. I was to hold down my fingers *and* the pedal for the appropriate length of time, and then lift off both together.

Similarly, I try to follow through on long marimba notes. After the attack, I try, whenever possible, to hold the mallet head over the bar for the correct length of time. I imagine that, by stopping the mallet head a short distance above the bar, I am physically trapping the sound waves, and causing the resonance to be more pronounced for a longer period. Admittedly, the effect is mostly visual but, in certain rooms/acoustics, I am sure that I have heard a discernible difference in the length of the note (and others have heard it too!). In any case, just like with the piano pedal, doing this keeps me much more engaged with the music.

Dynamics, touch, and weight of arm stroke can also be used to differentiate between note durations. To produce "weighty arm strokes," my strokes don't begin too much higher than my normal strokes; the difference is that I'm aware of my strokes beginning at my shoulder, with the weight of my arm exaggerating the tenuto stroke. This works well on heavy, main beats in certain styles of music.

You can also do this in one hand (and even, to some extent, one mallet, while the other mallet in that hand is subordinate) while using a normal stroke in the other hand. For instance, if in the right hand you were playing a melody in quarter notes and, in the left hand, a counterline in eighth notes, it would help to clarify the different voices as well as different note durations if you played the quarter notes very slightly louder and with a heavy, tenuto stroke (e.g., Section II, Study 22).

In Section IV, Handel's "Sarabande" and Hasse's "Bow Bells" provide opportunities to play very full, resonant chords (and practice your tenuto stroke). Chopin's "Prélude" offers much more involved challenges in terms of differentiating between different note durations.

Stroke Preparation

Your tone will always be fuller and warmer if your mallets are in position, ready to play, if for only a split second, before you need to. In contrast, if you rush to reach a note and strike it the very moment you arrive, the sound quality will be a bit slappy and harsh. Being at the note(s) before you need to play particularly improves the tone quality of long and/or loud notes. It's a good general guideline for all your playing; being in position to play every note before you need to will also improve your focus and note accuracy.

Body Positioning

Don't hesitate to change your body position if it will put you at a better angle to play an awkward interval. For example, if you need to play B, D, F-sharp and A, it's quite awkward if you're standing right in front of the chord because of the angle of your right wrist (which is contorted in order to play the F-sharp and A, even if you play the F-sharp on the edge beating spot). If you take a small step to the left (or even keep your feet in the same place and just shift your weight to the left side), your right wrist will be in a much more comfortable position while playing the F-sharp and A. This shift will compromise all your beating spots slightly, but try to compensate and mitigate this as much as possible.

In some cases you might have to play the same set of notes (B, D, F-sharp and A) and not have time to shift your body to the left as described above. Then, the secret to your right wrist not looking terribly awkward is to pretend it isn't awkward! Hopefully, you can get in and out of this position quickly. Try to bend your wrist *only* to play the awkward interval, without hitching up your shoulder and/or tensing your arm.

Dynamic Levels

I find it very helpful to think in terms of having a certain basic, physical posture for each basic dynamic level. In particular, this helps when I need to play at one dynamic plateau for a stretch of time. It makes me feel more free to be expressive—that is, add certain musical nuances—yet feel confident that I will remain within certain dynamic parameters.

If a musical passage is marked ***p***, my basic physical approach might be to be a bit crouched, *working* to be quite gentle. (It takes effort to play ***p***!) Take care that your ***p***s are not too soft! Because the marimba can be played so softly, people often underplay ***p***s. But at ***p***, your tone should have significant presence.

Having a certain kind of physical stance in mind for playing ***p*** can really help to distinguish that dynamic level from other surrounding levels. For instance, by contrast to the basic posture I think of when I'm playing ***p***, I would physically feel much more like I am "tip-toeing" or "walking on eggshells" when I need to play ***pp***. (That takes even more effort!) To me, ***pp*** means the sound can begin to lack presence and be somewhat distant. By ***ppp*** that is very much the case; the sound is very much "under wraps" and hushed: barely there.

Working toward the louder spectrum of dynamics, I think of my stance at ***mp*** as quite relaxed. At ***mf*** I'm still relaxed, but in a little more robust state of being. The weight of my arm movements naturally plays into the dynamic (so that, in contrast to playing quietly, it actually takes less effort to play more loudly).

Of course, appropriate dynamic levels are a relative thing. You must be sensitive to others with whom you're playing, your environment (the room or hall), the acoustics, how close to you people are seated, and sometimes the type of people who comprise your audience. Therefore, these postures will frequently shift, depending on your situation.

In terms of holding the mallets, at soft dynamics I am quite aware of nuances of pressure in my fingertips. At louder dynamics, I am more aware of anchoring the mallets in the back of my hand.

Be careful with *diminuendos* in soft dynamics; I often hear players overdo *diminuendos*. Because it is easy to play softly on the marimba, people sometimes get too soft. If, for instance, you roll on a long chord and *diminuendo*, it is very important to be aware of the point at which the sound loses presence relative to the acoustics in which you're playing. If you dip below that level, the chord will not sound as if it has been played the appropriate duration. If you want to end a roll by disappearing, save it for the *very* end—maybe just the last second. This is one of those instances in which marimbists can get carried away by how "cool" it *feels* to play softly, but the music will be meaningless if it can't be heard.

Playing Loudly

I'm not a very strong person physically. In order to play ***f*** and ***ff***, I need to think about power reserves I can utilize in my body to help create and support loud dynamics.

What helps the most is to utilize my back muscles. Whenever I see a loud passage coming, I flex my back muscles in preparation. This gives me a firm basis—a kind of anchor—for the forward energy I need to exert. These muscles are in the area of my shoulder blades, below them, and slightly in toward my sides (under my arms). To flex them, imagine that you are trying to bring your shoulder blades together, but without the aid of pushing back your elbows/arms.

To some extent, I also get power from my shoulders and upper arms. When I play very loudly for an extended period, I know my neck may tense up a bit, too. To avoid injury, I think the important thing is to be aware that you may stress these areas *before* you play loudly and, as much as possible, to flex your back so that the brunt of the exertion is absorbed there rather than in your shoulders and neck.

A cautionary word about playing the marimba loudly. For those marimbists who *are* physically strong, as well as for those who are not and may utilize my advice above, beware that it is very easy to overplay the marimba! My father (who, for some reason, has taken to listening to a lot of marimba playing… I wonder why?!) points out what a lovely, glorious tone the marimba possesses. It is the reason most of us are attracted to the instrument. Yet, my father and I hear so many people cross the line and overpower it. The result goes against the marimba's very nature and accounts for quite an ugly sound. He astutely points out that players ought to concentrate on "finding, by trial and error, the limit of one's particular keyboard, and then learn how to maintain that limit while performing with all desired shadings."

Interestingly, he noted that his concern for players overpowering the marimba "does not apply to orchestral marimba playing, which simply never calls for such violent mallet-striking that solo performers [sometimes] use in their interpretation of a given piece." When the marimba is occasionally utilized in orchestral music, it is the instrument's characteristic mellow sound that is desired and explored.

In solo playing, he often hears players become quite violent and play at a level that is a "sound-killer." He recognizes they are carried away in pursuit of expressing musical emotions but, again, they have crossed a line. On the other side of that line is percussion. It may be controversial that I use the term disparagingly (when it is the marimba's "family"), but sometimes I feel my life's work, in a nutshell, has been to separate the marimba from percussion.

When the marimba is played too loudly, it becomes difficult or impossible to discern the pitch that was played. Since it is by nature a pitched instrument—and the quality of a marimba is always defined by the nature and richness of its tone—it seems ludicrous to me to think that it's acceptable to sometimes ignore sound quality.

It is alarming how matter-of-fact marimbists as a group are about breaking marimba bars. At some marimba competitions, certain manufacturers supply a huge case of replacement bars, and expect they will need to replace broken bars at many intervals throughout each day of the competition. This is madness! If that level of breakage occurred to some part of any other instrument, people would be shocked and horrified by its misuse by the performer(s). To me, understanding and respecting the marimba's dynamic limits is part of playing it well, and another facet that could dramatically elevate the marimba's stature; if marimbists approached the instrument with greater respect, so might the public.

Applying These Ideas

Use your imagination. Articulations will sometimes be marked, but oftentimes are not. You can opt to apply them to create more character and variety in your playing, depending on what seems appropriate. The same goes for what beating spots you choose to use for timbral effects, and whether or not to occasionally angle your mallets.

The most important factor in deciding whether or not to make use of these devices is whether you feel they make a difference in how sensitively you can play, and whether you hear and enjoy a difference when you use them. (I utilized many of the articulation ideas in the course of working and performing with Sharan Leventhal in Marimolin. We were frequently faced with a new piece that was full of articulation and tone directives for the violinist, but which offered none for me. It challenged me to continually experiment to see if I couldn't emulate some of the effects my partner was able to achieve on the violin.)

Playing the marimba is very physical. As you develop your technique, it's natural to be drawn to thinking about your movements. This is important in order to learn and build good habits to move in healthy ways. But beware of the danger inherent in some technical "tricks." Percussionists as a group can get way too easily sucked in to focusing on what they're *doing*, rather than *the sound they are making*.

I've gone into quite a bit of detail about how I relate strokes and tone production in physical ways, yet, in reality, I think very little about what I'm doing physically. Everything mentioned here—and other physical devices you may invent for yourself—is ridiculous if it doesn't serve the music.

Listen to yourself. Listen as objectively as possible. *The most important thing is the sound you produce and whether it feels genuinely musical and meaningful.*

3B Relationship of Sticking Choices to Phrasing

Phrasing vs. Pulse

"Presto" from J.S. Bach's "Sonata N° 1 in G minor for Unaccompanied Violin"

A good example of a sticking that relates beautifully to phrasing is shown below for the opening descending arpeggio of the "Presto" from J.S. Bach's "Sonata N° 1 in G minor for Unaccompanied Violin." The piece is in 3/8 time, yet the contour of the notes in the opening three (or four) measures falls most naturally into groups of three sixteenth notes: two per bar. My opinion is that if Bach wanted the music to be felt in two beats per bar, he would have written the meter as 6/16. Since he wrote 3/8, I like to emphasize three beats per bar.

My ideal is to subtly highlight *both* the triple pulse and duple phrases. This can be accomplished by a series of "LRR" stickings ("244" etc. amounts to the same), which enable my left hand to easily, consistently play with slightly more weight (in order to distinguish the groupings of three sixteenth notes). At the same time, I can superimpose a sense of the 3/8 pulse by slightly emphasizing the notes that fall on each beat. (Note that if I changed every 3 or 4 sticking marked below to simply R, and every 1 or 2 sticking to an L, it would work perfectly with two mallets.)

When I play with four mallets, I feel quite comfortable alternating between hands (using occasional double-stickings) and, on a smaller level, alternating between which mallet I use in those hands, when it results in minimizing my movements. Not everyone is comfortable doing this. If you aren't comfortable with so much shifting within your hands, feel free to simplify the stickings in the following example to more continually use the same mallet in each hand. (I would suggest 2 and 4 most of the time; so this means you would change some or all of the 1's to 2's, and the 3's to 4's, keeping the others as they are.)

Every phrase—including those which aren't marked but that are suggested by the contour of the notes—as well as most measures, begin with a "clean hand" (a note that is *not* the second note of a double-sticking; but *do* use double-stickings to *set up* a "clean hand" to play important notes [see the end of Section I-J. Basics of Good Phrasing]). The only exception, which was unavoidable, given the contour of the notes, is the last sixteenth note of mm. 12–15 and the following downbeat (when the downbeats don't occur with a "clean hand").

Notice that many of the main beats and phrases that begin with a "clean hand" were set up by a double-sticking preceding the important note. While I advocate hand-to-hand alternations, I don't like to alternate to the point that I need to cross my mallets when I get to the highest or lowest notes in the phrase. Generally, I always play the highest note of a phrase with my right hand (and definitely mallet 4 on very high notes), and the lowest note of a phrase with my left hand (mallet 1 on very low notes). I advocate getting very comfortable with double-stickings. Ian Finkel taught me a fabulous two-mallet exercise for working on this, which carries over well into four-mallet playing (see below).

The point of all of this is to keep your torso as relaxed as possible. This will keep you most open to ways you can use the weight of your arms (stemming from your shoulders), as well as strength reserves supported by your back, to create the impression that more than one stroke "falls out" of one arm movement. This can add tremendous fluidity and lilt to your playing. In the case of the "Presto," try to make it feel as if each bar "falls out" of one stroke.

Double-Sticking Exercise

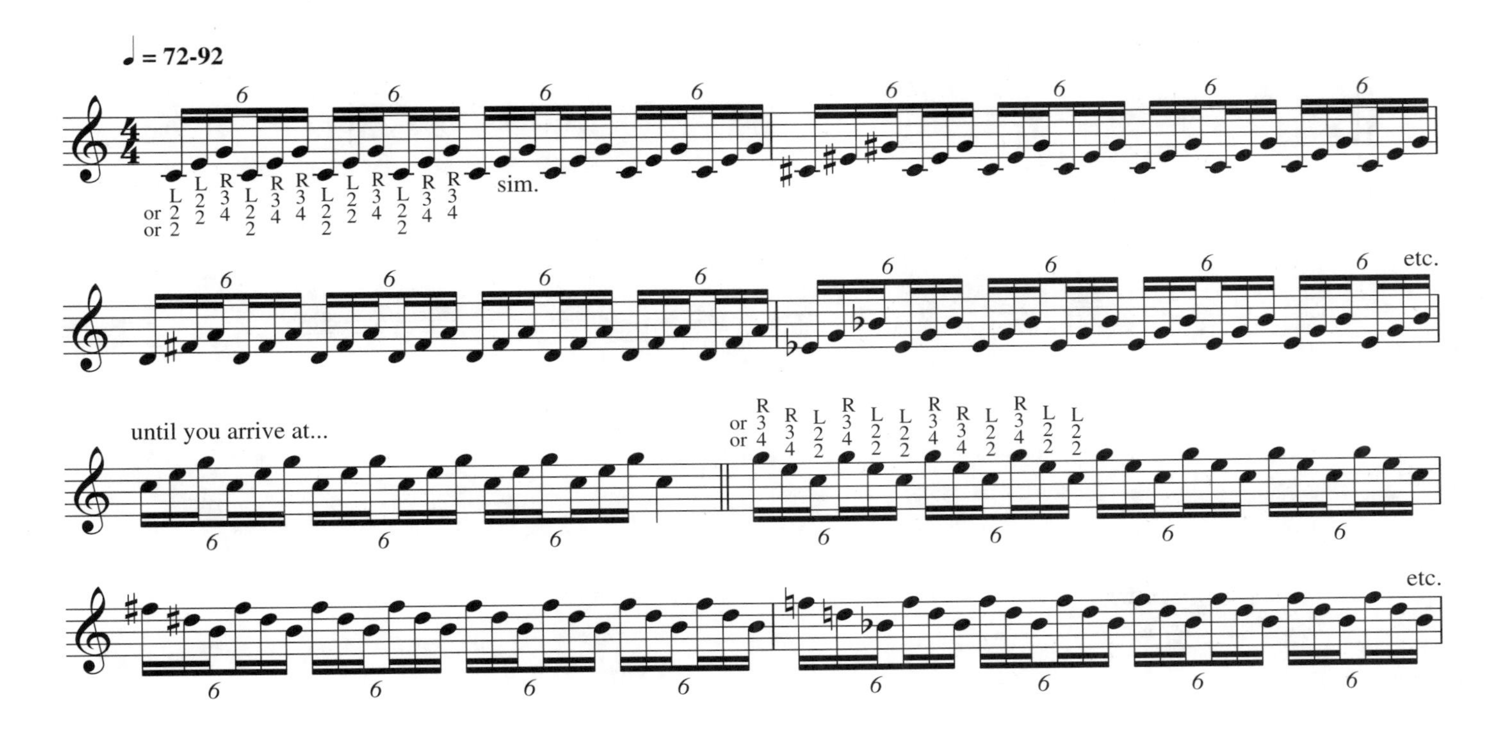

Your goal with this exercise should be to keep your mallets low at all times, and to work on your sideways throw between the double-sticked pairs of notes. Ultimately, the ones that are awkward (because of particular configurations of "black" and "white" notes) should sound as smooth as all the easier ones (which lie between two black or two white notes). You should also work to dynamically balance each three-note grouping so that they have a uniform loping, "waltzy" feel, no matter which sticking was used.

Avoid Triple-Stickings

"Prelude 21, B-flat Major" from Bach's *The Well-Tempered Clavier, Book I*

In most playing, it will become fairly standard for you to use double-stickings for the reasons described above. But I suggest you avoid triple-stickings, that is, three successive notes played with the same hand. Sometimes there are no other solutions and, when the tempo isn't too fast, they can work out fine. (Of course there are instances in which you must play many successive notes in one mallet in contrapuntal playing, or situations in which you might play a succession of slow notes with one mallet in order to control and match each stroke.)

The particular type of triple-stickings I want to caution against are often applied to the following Bach "Prelude." Many have played this piece, and other pieces with a similar note configuration, using the sticking 2343, 2343, etc. (or, later in the piece, 1343). I feel this is extremely dangerous—a recipe for tendonitis! It is unnatural to begin a wrist rotation (as with the 2343 sticking), "freeze" it, and then begin another, as opposed to completing the rotation, which occurs with a one-handed roll. Because of the type of concentrated control it requires, the figures tend to lack a flowing sense of phrasing and, instead, sound quite robotic.

A *much* more comfortable and healthy sticking in situations such as this is 1243, 1243, etc. With this sticking, the music will sound much more beautifully phrased. The 1243 configuration comprises balanced, symmetrical movements that lend themselves to flowing, natural-feeling phrasing.

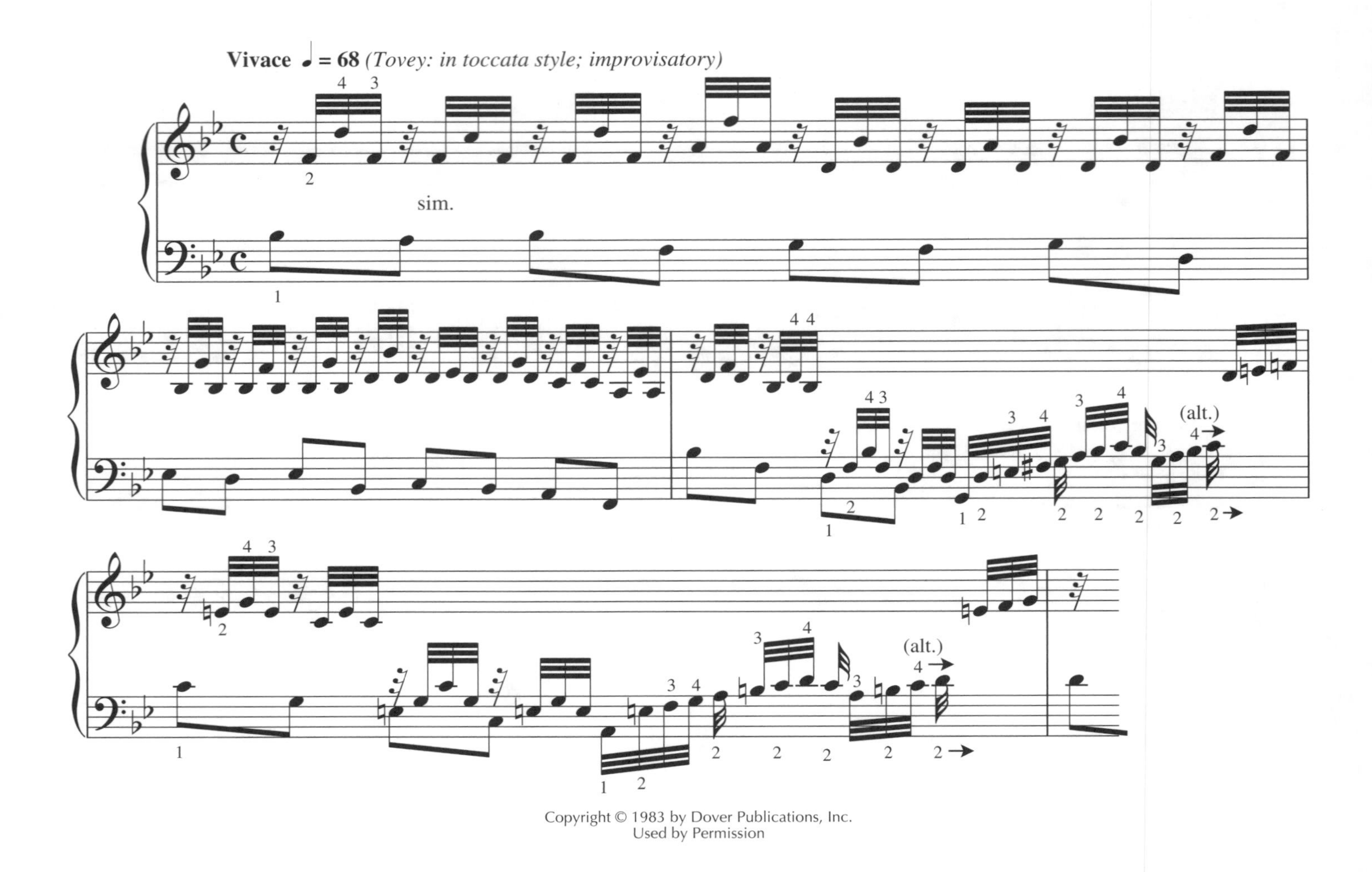
Vivace ♩ = 68 (Tovey: in toccata style; improvisatory)
sim.
(alt.)
(alt.)

Measure 2, admittedly, is quite challenging using the 1243 sticking. On the first beat, avoid hitching up your right shoulder to play the awkward intervals (G and B-flat, then F and B-flat); instead, concentrate on keeping your shoulder relaxed and getting in position to play the first few groupings as early as possible. I would approach playing the wide intervallic leaps in the left hand by spreading my mallets as wide as possible and using sideways wrist throws between the notes. If you can master this – maintaining beautiful dynamic control and shaping of each eighth-note grouping – you will also have achieved lovely phrasing. (It could be fine to occasionally use the 1343 sticking in m. 2 if you prefer it, but it should be the exception not the rule.)

Marimba playing, obviously, is comprised of vertical strokes. The more we can camouflage that fact, the more smooth and elegant our playing can sound. The sideways wrist throws (here, as well as those inherent in the double-stickings advocated above) contribute a wonderful "horizontal" approach to covering the keyboard, which results in a legato sound.

Sticking to Enhance Phrasing

"Prelude" from Bach's "Suite N° 1" from *Six Suites for Violoncello Solo*

This piece provides excellent examples of how I apply many of the sticking objectives described in this book. My choice of stickings is always based on those that will enhance phrasing, "lay well," and set up "clean hands." These stickings may seem complicated at first but, in fact, they spring from my desire to meet the latter criteria using minimal movement. I hope you will find them to be comfortable, and gain some new ideas from them. (It's not necessary to follow absolutely every sticking indicated; you could certainly change a few if you discover some stickings that are more comfortable for you.)

When I begin to study a new piece, I take into account the above considerations and, for the sake of efficiency, fairly early in the learning process decide on stickings that will benefit my priorities, and I adhere to them. Of course, I sometimes make amendments when a sticking continually poses problems, or I find myself continually drawn to a different maneuver. I usually write down the minimum stickings necessary to remind me what I want to do, so my music doesn't become too cluttered. (Here I have rather heavily notated stickings to ensure that my intentions are clear.)

A quick tour of my rationales behind some of these choices:

- m. 1, beat 2: the "4 3" prepares you to play the next important bass note with a clean hand.
- m. 3, beat 2: the "4 3" on the C and F-sharp is a bit awkward. Move your body (or even just shift your body weight) to the left in order to lessen this. I would also use the edge beating spot on the F-sharp.
- m. 5, beat 4: I suggest the edge beating spot for the C-sharp.
- m. 6, beat 1: I suggest the center beating spot (for mallet 1) on the C-sharp.
- m. 7, beat 1: I chose this double-sticking (which still enables you to start with a clean hand) because the register is higher. Using graduated mallets, I prefer the tone of mallet 2 in this register (to my bass mallet).
- mm. 7–14: I use all edge beating spots on the black keys. This sections needs more clarity of pitch and playing that feels at ease than it needs resonance. (The same goes for many upcoming passages.)
- m. 15 and 20: I would use the middle beating spot on the downbeats of these measures, since the bass note should be resonant. (The same goes for most bass notes.)
- m. 22, beat 4 and m. 23, beat 2: In scalar passages beginning with mallets 2 and 3, sometimes a good place to switch to mallets 2 and 4 is on a "black" note, as is the case with the F-sharp here. (The payoff is being able to play the top note of the phrases with mallet 4.)
- m. 31–38: When the music/phrasing is simple and straightforward, I like for the stickings to be also.

Prelude

from Suite I of
Six Suites for Violoncello Solo

Johann Sebastian Bach
(composed about 1720)

BACH SIX SUITES FOR VIOLONCELLO SOLO (FR. SCHIRMER'S LIBRARY OF MUSICAL CLASSICS)
Revised and Edited by Frits Gaillard

*Use mallets 2 and 4 if you decide to roll this note.

More Guidelines

1. Generally avoid convoluted, "clever" stickings that disrupt the flow of notes between hands. If a sticking strikes you as a "good exercise," it may very well not be the most musical choice. Ultimately, I intend for my stickings to exhibit common sense and not seem unduly complicated.
2. Always try to recognize which mallets could be used in order for you to move around as little as possible. Think in terms of minimal movement both in terms of keeping your mallet heads low and moving your body as little as possible.
3. In deciding where to use double-stickings, consider that the "falling off" motion of moving from a "black note" to an adjacent "white note" is very comfortable. At the same time, don't necessarily rule out double-stickings from a "white note" to a "black note." (The Double-Sticking Exercise above will help you become more comfortable with these.)
4. Seldom play chords with stickings that don't use the mallets in consecutive order (that is, 1 for the lowest note to 4 for the highest note). Keeping the voices in the same consecutive order of your mallets will improve the balance of chords you play, especially if you use graduated mallets, which will also improve how you phrase chords within melodic lines.
5. Consider phrasing issues, and try to play phrases thoughtfully, from the first moment you look at a piece.

Refining Rolls

Before studying this section, I recommend reviewing Section I-G. Basic Rolls.

Sustaining

In any situation in which you are asked to roll, ask yourself, "Are these rolls here because it's desirable to have notes with roll texture, or because these notes are to be sustained?" In the majority of instances, a roll is a device for sustaining and, in those cases, it is advisable to minimize the roll texture in favor of a smooth, resonant sustain.

For most people whose goal is to sustain, just *thinking* about that will make your rolls sound smoother. The reason is that it will make you listen harder and more objectively to what rolls really sound like. (Rolling is another instance in which marimbists tend to get caught up in what they're *doing*, which may compromise how they're *sounding*.)

We enjoy the smooth sustains available on the piano through use of the pedal. The richness of the sound becomes the focal point and pulls our attention away from another characteristic of the piano: the dynamic drop-off between the attack of notes and their pedaled sustain. But this is a phenomenon that marimbists should more often try to reproduce.

If you play an ***f*** chord, followed by a ***p*** roll, it is really quite convincing that you are not rolling on the ***p*** chord, just sustaining. Experiment with how much you can narrow the difference between the attack dynamic and sustain dynamic and still have the sense of sustain dominate over awareness of roll texture. Hopefully, you will be able to develop the ability to, for instance, strike an ***mf*** chord in a resonant register of the marimba (all four notes together, with a nice tenuto stroke) and then roll at "***mf*** –" or ***mp*** with the impression that the sustain is much smoother (that is, the roll texture is minimized). It will still sound ***mf*** because of the continuing resonance. Essentially, you're trying to "get inside" the resonance and extend it.

Breathing With Rolls

Breathing with rolls is incredibly important. It is intrinsically tied to phrasing and how you would sustain pitches if you were singing. If you play a chorale (rolled four-note chords) with all the right notes, in a steady tempo, with smooth shifting between notes, correct dynamics, and an interesting variety of roll speeds, but fail to breathe with it, your playing is likely to sound empty or somehow lacking.

Rolling, even on one note, when its purpose is to sustain, is supposed to create a concentration of sound. I don't believe you can create a truly concentrated sound without breathing with it in order to support it. With richer harmonies (rolls on two to four notes) the concentration of sound is even more intense.

What I mean by breathing with your playing and supporting it is a combination of feeling in your throat at least a "shadow" of how it would feel to sing a passage, as well as relating your normal inhalations and exhalations to subtly different combinations of events that frequently occur in music: tension and release, swelling and relaxation, forward momentum and resolution, pushing and stretching, urgency and calmness. Music, when it's going well, is alive. We are alive because we breathe.

Generally, you might inhale as a line *crescendos* or maintains intensity, and exhale as a phrase *diminuendos* or maintains a sense of simplicity. Musical lines are almost always moving in some direction—or purposefully not moving. (There is a certain intensity of focus necessary to maintain a monotone or steady dynamic level, just as there would be in singing at a flat level.)

Imagine that your rolls are not just happening at the marimba, but that the sound you create is entering your chest, being energized in your wind column, and coming out through your hands. Also visualize the air pressure your playing is creating to force the sounds through the marimba's resonator tubes—the air columns of the marimba. Sometimes you will just breathe normally as you roll, but you still need to be aware that the movement of air is tied to the sustain you're creating (just as it is for a singer or wind player). Breathing is at the heart of everything we do that is smooth or graceful. The essence of how we intake air and draw nourishment from it is rich, complete, and satisfying. So, when it comes to sustain—a smooth, rich, personal creation—it makes a lot of sense to rely on the guidance available in our breathing.

Legato Rolls

Shifting pitches smoothly while rolling can be quite difficult. This is equally true of rolling on single notes as moving between chords. Many people tend to speed up their rolls just before an awkward shift, probably out of anxiety, a desire to maintain intensity, and in the hopes of filling the gap between notes. It works sometimes, but can be risky if your alternations sputter out of control or, if in your hysteria, you accidentally include some wrong notes.

One of my tricks for achieving smoothness is to try to do the opposite. When an awkward shift approaches, especially if it is very exposed, I make a conscious effort to slightly slow down the speed of my hand alternations. There's a good chance it will keep me calmer and more focused and, moreover, create the illusion of smoothness because there is no disruption within my hand alternations.

In rolling a single-line melody using four mallets, you can make your connections between notes more legato by using what I call "eentsy-weentsy-spider stickings." (This refers to the nursery rhyme in which you show children how a spider climbs up the web he spins by connecting the tip of your left thumb to the tip of your right second finger and pivoting on them so that, higher in the air, you can next connect the tip of your left second finger to the tip of your right thumb, and so on.) In the children's finger game, you pivot and prepare to make the next connection before you let go of the previous one. Similarly, if you choose your stickings wisely, you can get prepared to use certain combinations of mallets before you need to play with them and, therefore, make very legato connections between rolls. Studies 19 and 25 in Section II demonstrate this.

Balancing Chords

When rolling three- and four-note chords, it is extremely important that you are sensitive to balancing the notes within them. This means you are aware of each pitch, and listening carefully to the presence of each pitch within your roll texture. At the same time, concentrate on how the notes within each chord blend together. There should be the sense that the various individual tones become "homogenized" into a new entity.

In some cases you may wish to bring out a certain voice. (Studies 12, 31 and 50 specifically require this.) First, practice playing a chord in which all the notes are played at an equal dynamic. Then, hold the chord emphasizing the soprano voice. Continue to hold the chord emphasizing the alto voice, then the tenor voice, and then the bass voice. With traditional grip, this requires a little extra finger pressure on the mallet you

want to bring out, as well as lightening your touch on the mallet you want to de-emphasize within the same hand.

It's important in all chorale playing to make clear which voice(s) is (are) prominent. If there is some "conversation" between voices, I try to bring attention to the moving voices. Frequently, this means that I play some chords trying to balance the notes equally, then try to subtly bring out the voice that is going to move (to draw attention to it) just before the change to the new pitch.

Types of Rolls and Variations

One possibility for expressiveness with the "2+2" roll (described in I-G. Basic Rolls) comes with varying the speed of your alternations. Occasionally playing them extremely open and suddenly moving toward more rapid alternations can be quite effective. (Gordon Stout is the master of this!) Sometimes this can sound rather stilted at close range, but in a hall with nice acoustics, it can sound wonderful.

With the ripple roll (also introduced in I-G. Basic Rolls), there are additional possible ripple configurations, such as 1234, 4321, and 3421, which is the same as 2134. (I have never bothered to practice these other configurations, but it couldn't hurt, if it interests you to do so.)

The "split-bar" or "mandolin" roll is a technique in which, with the right hand, you play at the edge of the bar with mallet 3 above the bar and mallet 4 below the bar, rolling with a vertical motion. It is easiest for me if my hand position rotates outward so that my thumb faces up. I hold the mallets quite firmly with my fourth and fifth fingers, which allows them to be held quite loosely between the first, second, and third fingers. (The left hand would play a split-bar roll with mallet 2 above the bar and mallet 1 below the bar.)

The split-bar roll technique can sometimes replace one-handed rolls on "white" notes that are awkward to reach. But they tend to sound slightly different than regular one- or two-handed rolls. Each mallet head striking from above or below the edge of the bar doesn't have far to move and can have a slight dampening effect. The other reason for a compromise in tone quality is that you are not playing on ideal beating spots. Therefore, I tend to use them sparingly unless they are specifically called for, or unless I'm going for a unique timbre.

One-handed rolls are quite common and, for some, quite challenging, so I have devoted the next chapter to them. Occasionally you may need to play double (that is, simultaneous) one-handed rolls (for example, Section II, Study 45, mm. 11–14). I find these sound best if you try to roll in each hand at slightly different speeds (usually faster in the right hand on higher pitches); when all the mallets hit at a different time, the sustain sounds smoother.

One-Handed Rolls

I believe in approaching one-handed rolls from a standpoint of relaxation as opposed to muscle-building. At the heart of my relaxed approach is "wiggling." The more technical approach often centers around exercises in which alternated strokes between the two mallets of one hand are practiced in measured rhythms. Certainly both methods can produce good results, depending on the individual.

Wiggling

Stand squarely in front of the marimba and, with one hand at a time, prepare to play a comfortable-sized interval: maybe a fifth or sixth. In practicing wiggling, you will be targeting *approximately* those notes but, in the beginning, it doesn't matter if you occasionally hit some neighboring notes.

Begin to wiggle your arm. The mallet heads will flop around crazily; this is fine. Try to stay loose. Wiggle fairly quickly. It's fine to wiggle in various directions, and sometimes in more than one direction at a time. Then, gradually, while staying relaxed, try to begin to control the wiggle into a sideways rotation (the same kind of rotation as I described the inner mallets use when playing independently within traditional grip).

Begin to think about the pivot point (for the sideways rotations). For me, it is almost halfway between my wrist and elbow. Related to the circumference of my arm, it's halfway between the middle of the top of my arm and the side of my arm (that is, over the radius bone). Imagine that you are a marionette, and your puppeteer's string links to your arm at this point. Stay loose, and imagine you are pivoting left and right from this "string point."

Willing It to Work

A wonderful trick for being able to do one-handed rolls has to do with "willing it to work." After you've tried for a while to wiggle, and you're able to accomplish some semblance of a roll, take a break. With one mallet in each hand, play a simple roll with two hands on the same interval as before. This is how you want your one-handed roll to sound!

Keep remembering how it sounded when you rolled with both hands, as you try again to roll (wiggle) with one hand. Ninety-percent of people suddenly can play a great-sounding one-handed roll, if only for two seconds; but it's a start! Once you see that you can

actually do it for two seconds, you can keep building on that. Study what you're doing when it works well. See which hand can do it more easily, study why, and get your other hand to copy it.

It's a good idea, even once you are competent with one-handed rolls, to take breaks and roll with two hands the notes you want to be able to roll in one hand. Two-handed rolls almost always sound better than one-handed rolls (because there tends to be a hint of note-dampening inherent in one-handed rolls). The clearer the image is in your mind of how you want your one-handed rolls to sound, the better chance you will have of matching it.

First Applications

I suggest learning one-handed rolls by practicing wiggling—and intermittently clarifying your goal by playing the roll with two hands—for fairly short periods. Try it for fifteen minutes a day, or two fifteen-minute segments separated by other practice. Never practice past the point you feel fatigued.

The best initial application for one-handed rolls is doing them in short bursts: situations in which there is the need for just an occasional one-handed roll. Studies 16, 37, 41, and 50 in Section II fit the bill. (Later, try the more demanding pieces utilizing one-handed rolls: Studies 34, 36, 42, and 45.)

Refinements

When you play a one-handed roll on one note, it usually works best to turn your arm so that it is almost parallel to the length of the marimba. You can then position the mallet heads so that the two beating spots are above the sides of the resonator tube. When the mallet heads are very close like this, the one-handed roll is quite difficult, since your hand rotations (wiggle) must be rather frenzied. An alternative would be to spread the mallets a little, so that one head is over the center of the resonator and the other is near the edge of the bar. With the mallets spread, your wiggle can be more relaxed, which many people find more comfortable.

The same is true for one-handed rolls on small intervals. Experiment with different angles at which you can play them. If keeping your mallet heads right over the resonator is uncomfortable (because of the pronounced wiggle required), then try turning your wrist (depending on the notes) so that you're playing at an angle, with one mallet head above one side of the resonator tube and the other above the other side of the tube. Or you can have one mallet head over the center of the bar, and one at the edge.

When playing one-handed rolls on mid-sized intervals, the third finger can help by cradling the outer mallet. On a larger scale, your elbow (and how you distribute your body weight behind the arm doing the one-handed roll) can also play a supportive role. It's helpful to position your elbow, *gracefully*, so that it is centered between the mallets, supporting your pivot point; but try not to have your elbow protrude awkwardly. (Players who use Stevens' Grip, who must cope with more mallet length because of holding the mallets at the ends, often have difficulty avoiding very angular positions with their elbows sticking out.) Especially in calm, delicate passages, you run the risk of your body positioning looking at odds with the mood of the music.

Playing one-handed rolls at loud, or even medium-level, dynamics can be quite challenging. While they still rely on the principle of wiggling, they also require the use of forearm muscles. Beyond that, I am conscious of supporting loud one-handed rolls using my back muscles, as described in Section III-A. Refining Strokes and Tone Production, Playing Loudly.

Gradually, over time, I developed increased control over my one-handed roll wiggle, and I learned to play every interval from every angle at a wide range of dynamics. To be honest, I had trouble doing one-handed rolls in pressured situations at first. If I was nervous and shaking a little, either I might get lucky and turn it into a wiggle, or everything might completely fall apart. But (knock on wood!), I'm now rather confident that those troubles are behind me. The key to success has been developing the ability to maintain focus on how I want my rolls to sound.

3E Refining Mallet Selection

Your Mallet Collection

You need about three basic sets of mallets that combine well and with which you love to play. They should feel good in your hands—that is, the weight of the heads, and the balance and finish of the handles—and, most importantly, you should love the sound they produce. That sound is "your voice."

Your collection could grow to include some mallets with a different head shape or weight; ones made with a different type of yarn (or differently-wrapped yarn); ones that are a bit worn and, therefore, more articulate; ones that are much harder or softer than you generally use (but which might occasionally be useful); and some unwrapped latex mallets. These will enable you to sometimes augment your general sound-world to encompass a broader spectrum of colors and effects. Some of the changes these mallets create are subtle; some are dramatic. This can be particularly welcome in the context of playing an entire recital, to add interest and showcase the marimba's versatility.

Graduated Mallets

My three basic sets of mallets are not matched sets of four; they're a collection of mixed mallets—something like one Encore NZ7, one NZ6, one NZ5, two NZ4s, two NZ3s, two old NZ3s, two NZ2s, and one old NZ2. My mallet bag almost never contains four mallets of any one kind—only one, two or three of each.

The initial inspiration for me to experiment with graduated mallets sprang from falling in love with playing a five-octave (low-C) marimba and realizing that making it sound good was much more complicated than making a low-A marimba sound good. There's a reason those last several notes cost so much more; it's difficult to get a piece of wood to be able to produce a beautiful low tone, and the challenge doesn't stop once it's been built.

I came to realize that, when the bars in the lowest octave were not played with rather soft mallets, the effect (especially in a concert hall) was that the lowest octave sounded very much like the octave above it. Medium-hard mallets, when used in the low register, tend to accentuate the upper harmonic partials of the bar. This meant I was enjoying the idea and act of playing a bigger instrument, but not really succeeding in making it *sound* bigger.

Further reinforcement that softer mallets made the fundamental pitches clearer came from my duo partner at the time, violinist Sharan Leventhal (in Marimolin). In chamber music, other instrumentalists frequently have difficulty tuning accurately to the marimba because the attack pitch often differs slightly from the pitch of the resonance. But Sharan was very accepting of the marimba's idiosyncrasies and determined to tune to me as precisely as possible. Especially in very harmonically complex music (like Schuller's "Phantasmata"; see Section V), the more often I used soft bass mallets, the easier it was for Sharan to tune to me. (Schuller was also adamant that softer mallets were critical to achieve the fundamental pitches he depended on hearing in order for his harmonies to sound as he intended.)

The line of eight graduated mallets I helped Encore Mallets develop is predicated on the concept that about seven different kinds of mallets are needed to best flatter the various registers of the marimba (the eighth mallet is a specialty mallet, to be described later). They certainly can overlap but, basically, if you play the notes within the lowest minor 6th of a five-octave marimba with an NZ7, and within the next minor 6th with an NZ6, and so on, you would hear what I believe is the ideal, rich tone that can be produced for each pitch.

My ideal is a dark, rich sound—but that may not be your ideal! Personally, I am attracted to the marimba for its mellowness and, generally, I try to downplay any resemblance it bears to a xylophone. In fact, I very rarely use an NZ1 mallet even though, according to my schematic in the paragraph above, NZ1 would be used for the entire top octave. (I frequently use the NZ2 for the top octave-and-a-half.) On the other end of the spectrum, I realize that the NZ8 "boomer bass" mallet will rarely be of use. I requested that Encore include it in my series for those special situations in which you want a huge, gong-like bass sound, with almost no attack.

Compromise

Decisions on what mallets to use for a particular piece must be made on a case-by-case basis, by assessing the relative priority a specific composition gives to registers, articulation, mood, and so on. Mallet choices on marimba are very often a compromise because of the challenge to make the entire instrument sound good with one kind of mallet. For me, graduated mallets result in the least compromise when playing on a five-octave marimba. Some people might argue that they prevent a uniformity of tone, and that the latter would best be achieved by using four identical mallets.

However, my goal is uniformity of *quality* and, perhaps, "vivid personality" of tone. Part of the glory of a five-octave marimba is its size, as well as the various natural characters and colors of its different registers. Personally, I do not wish to hide these differences but, rather, to accentuate them. There are the deep bass notes, the rich tenor register, the singing mid-range, the bright mid-to-high soprano range, and the brilliant "sopranino" register. I think that flattering each one individually (as much as possible) helps to make the instrument sound as big as it is, and also helps it to be most convincing as a full-blown, serious, sublime instrument.

In selecting an assortment of mallets for a piece, I look for those that will best flatter the registers in which I need to play. But there are always compromises. When a piece covers a lot of the instrument, for instance, I would almost always choose to sacrifice a little brilliance in the upper registers for the satisfaction of being able to play rich bass notes. (The harmonic content of the music is always clearer if the fundamental building blocks, the bass notes, are clear.)

If there is a lot of *forte* playing in a piece, I usually choose medium rather than hard mallets with which I can play without fear of damaging the instrument. I want to feel free to really dig into loud passages in order for them to have the strongest effect musically, and still maintain a good tone. By contrast, if you try to play loud passages with hard mallets in an appropriate manner (so as not to break your bars!), your playing can look weak and sound thin, and will probably sacrifice some musical excitement.

The issue of sometimes alternating between two different mallets within a graduated set is not as difficult to cope with as many people imagine. For more on this, refer to the end of Section I-E. Basics of Four-Mallet Stickings.

Using graduated mallets, you need to be thoughtful about stickings; for instance, you would probably want to avoid using a bass mallet (presumably in the mallet 1 position) in the mid-high registers as it will not speak clearly. Therefore, you would work out your stickings so that only the upper three mallets were used in the upper registers (this is the case with almost all the stickings I provide for the Studies in Section II). The use of graduated mallets does open up certain possibilities for interesting stickings. For example, in the lower registers, you could use the harder mallets on light grace notes or pick-ups for which you want more clarity, then go to the rich bass mallet (1) for the main notes/beats when you want a fuller tone (see Section IV, "Los Paraguas," "rapido, con energia" entrance).

Matching Mallets to Marimbas

Marimbists are cursed or blessed, depending on your perspective, with a variety of marimba manufacturers each making instruments with individual characteristics. The variety of sound available is good in the sense people are likely to feel at home with one or another marimba. However, the lack of standardization of bar width and placement makes it difficult for players to shift from one brand to another.

The difficulty lies not only in terms of having to readjust to different keyboard layouts, but in terms of producing a good sound when playing on different brands of marimbas. With each type of marimba, there is a particular quality to the way in which the bars "speak" when played. By this I mean how quickly the bar responds to your touch, but it also relates to the nature of the resonance and the particular tone quality of the instrument. Each line of commercially produced mallets tends to sound best on a certain marimba (probably the marimba played by the artist who designed the mallets).

Some performers are accustomed to switching between different brands of marimbas and, to some extent, have learned the adjustments they need to make. I am not one of them. I have become so accustomed to playing on a Marimba One that, when I play on any other, I can only give you an idea of how I play. Sometimes, having to play on other instruments can't be avoided, but I encourage you, whenever possible, to play on the brand of instrument you prefer. To a large extent, I feel it's impossible to truly develop your own sound until you work with one instrument consistently.

Touch vs. Mallet Changes

"Touch" is a rather subtle thing. Every player has his or her own, but some have a rather magic ability to a create a truly special tone at the point the mallet head contacts the bar: some kind of unique physical sensitivity. In special cases in which touch is very refined (usually with rather advanced players), it can, in combination with various articulations, often replace the need to use many different types of mallets. The variations in sound are usually more subtle, but this approach can work.

Others prefer to rely on the directness of changing mallets to accomplish more dramatic shifts in tone color. Personally, I am attracted to using a fairly wide selection of mallets in addition to trying to achieve a variety of coloristic nuances through using different types of touch and articulations.

"Response" is an important factor in selecting mallets. Sometimes I might start out with a set of mallets that sound fine, but realize I have to work too hard to make them speak. If that is the case, I usually go to harder mallets, but I try to play more lightly with them. This can produce very beautiful, easy-speaking tones. In fact, I particularly love how hard mallets sound in very soft playing.

When you need to adjust to a concert hall or room in which you're unaccustomed to performing, try to listen to how your sound fills the room. If possible, have someone listen from the audience's perspective and describe the sound to you. (Bear in mind that the acoustics will get dryer when the room is filled with people.) If a hall is very resonant you might try to play more incisively or go to slightly harder mallets. In a dry hall you could try to play with more tenuto strokes. Sometimes you can successfully adjust your touch—as well as focus more attention on how you want your sound to project—in lieu of changing your mallets.

A word about wooden (birch or maple) vs. rattan handles. The same mallet head placed on a birch handle and a rattan handle will produce a slightly sweeter tone from the rattan-handled one. I concede this, yet personally prefer the feeling of playing with birch (although I occasionally use rattan). The lack of flexibility with the wood gives me more confidence that the head will go where I direct it. Some players are able to use both for certain effects.

In general, mallets with lightweight heads tend to produce a thin sound. One reason is that you need to be somewhat aware of the balance of a mallet and the weight of the head in order to relate to it with any special kind of touch. Some people prefer lighter mallets because they're more comfortable, but sound must be the primary guiding factor in your mallet selection.

3F Building a Personal Repertoire

Expanding the Existing Repertoire

Marimba repertoire is extremely limited relative to that of other concert instruments. Much of what exists offers clever technical challenges and/or is pleasant to listen to, but is not of a very high level of quality relative to, for instance, the piano music of Beethoven, Schumann, Chopin, Brahms, or Debussy. In fact, the entire repertoire for marimba available today does not begin to rival the piano catalog of any one of those composers.

Given that we have chosen to play an instrument in this predicament, I recommend that all marimbists help to remedy this situation by encouraging composers to write for the marimba. Ideally, you should be familiar with a composer's work before you approach him or her about composing a piece for you. Sometimes it's also helpful if you know a little about the composer personally, in order to gain a sense of whether you have compatible views on music. Through the particular composers we select to commission we can, to some degree, assert our personal tastes.

There are many other benefits of collaborations with composers. First, in describing to people how to write for the marimba, we learn about ourselves. We come to understand, and learn to articulate, our personal preferences in terms of technique, style, and approach to the instrument. For me, once composers have a clear idea of how to write idiomatically for the marimba, and a general sense of my relationship with the instrument, I am inclined to give them free reign, perhaps suggesting only an approximate length for the piece. My gut feeling is that the purest inspiration for my piece could result if they are mainly encouraged to "follow the muse."

It can be fascinating to work with composers as a piece is being written, or in preparation for its first performance. Oftentimes, certain details or sections that don't make sense initially seem perfectly plausible once a composer describes his or her musical intentions. Sometimes performers give composers useful feedback regarding notational devices that would put across their ideas more clearly. All this tends to change one's outlook on playing *all* music—even by composers with whom we cannot meet. One becomes more finely tuned to what could be intended through notation.

It's exciting to help establish the performance practice of the new piece. The inclusion of a premiere on your program makes it unique, and can stir up interest from the public and the press. You are making history!

Not every piece you encourage is going to be a "winner." You might very well just be adding to the pool of mediocre marimba music. But sometimes you will get lucky. In the big picture, commissioning is always a positive step. The more composers learn about writing for marimba, the more chances there are that the muse *will* strike, or that some young Chopin or Debussy will create a world of amazing music for the marimba.

Transcriptions

There is some controversy over whether adaptations of classical music are a good thing or not. Yes, some can be in bad taste (which is, of course, subjective), but I believe one can choose wisely.

Personally, I think transcriptions for marimba are a great idea. There are several reasons.

1. Since we face limited resources of good music composed for marimba, playing transcriptions increases our repertoire possibilities to include music that *is* of excellent quality.
2. Since most of the music for marimba was composed in the last fifty years or so, it doesn't represent a very broad range of styles (relative to the world of music). Marimbists will become much finer and better-rounded musicians by playing transcriptions which encompass music from all periods and styles.
3. The addition of transcriptions makes marimba recital programs more stylistically diverse, and probably more interesting to audiences.
4. Transcriptions encourage performers to exercise their imaginations and assert their personal tastes through their repertoire selections. They enhance each performer's individuality, and increase their chances of presenting more honest, intriguing programs—which hold the potential for more impact. The deeper the effect every marimbist has on an audience, the greater the chances of increasing the marimba's presence in the concert music world.

By advocating the playing of transcriptions on the marimba, I do not intend only to encourage the playing of J.S. Bach! There is no doubt that Bach composed gorgeous music, much of which translates beautifully to the marimba, but I feel that the practice of doing so has begun to be accepted to a bizarre degree, and is oftentimes the only exception made by those who are generally opposed to transcriptions. (International marimba competitions have required works by Bach in one or more rounds; why not Scarlatti, Mozart, Grieg or Bartòk? You might notice that, except for a few examples, this book is devoid of music by J.S. Bach. My choices in Section IV are meant to serve as suggestions for other possible directions to take.)

That said, the music of J.S. Bach that translates particularly well includes the sonatas and partitas for unaccompanied violin, the lute music, the suites for unaccompanied cello, and some of the *Two-Part Inventions, Well-Tempered Clavier*, and *French and English Suites* for keyboard. What I personally find most idiomatic (of the above list) are the violin pieces, played an octave lower than written. (Bach translated his own music between instruments rather freely, and I don't think he would be opposed to this!) What I personally find least idiomatic are the chorales. Many of them can work beautifully in the hands of competent players, but they are often misused in marimba teaching. They are often assigned to fairly inexperienced students as material to use in working on rolls, but they pose far too many challenges to serve that purpose well.

I would add rolls to any transcription with extreme caution. When it comes to translating sustains, I always try to take into account the effect that was achieved on the original instrument. Sometimes rolls can work if you really try to minimize the roll texture. Other times, there's no way to ignore that they add a strange texture that distorts the composer's intentions, and you'd be better off just letting the pitches ring (that is, using the marimba's natural sustain) or giving up on translating that piece to marimba altogether. In music that contains trills, be especially careful to differentiate between trills

and rolls. I often begin trills a bit slowly in order to bring attention to those figures, in contrast to the evenly-paced alternations of my rolls.

While I always try to respect and reproduce the effect of sustains as they were written for the original instrument, in some other regards I take a less "purist" approach. For example, if a piece is played quite slowly on violin because it is very difficult, and the piece sounds wonderful but is not quite as difficult on the marimba, it may flatter the piece and ultimately produce a more convincing musical effect if the piece is played a bit faster on the marimba in order to make the level of difficulty more relative to that of the piece played on violin. Another example is the issue of whether or not to ripple (that is, arpeggiate) or "break" chords that were written for violin and cello because of the fact that, on those instruments, the chords must be broken in bowing across the strings. (Actually, the bridges of Baroque string instruments were flatter than on their modern counterparts and more conducive to chordal playing.) My opinion is, break them if you like the effect of the "fat" sound that achieves on marimba; but, if you prefer the notes played together, since you can on marimba, go ahead and do so! (Again, I have the feeling Bach, for one, would smile down upon an open approach to this.)

There is an art to making good transcriptions. In some cases, pieces translate very easily and naturally to the marimba. In other cases, they can work if you use some imagination. Oftentimes, the deciding factor is whether the natural length of sustain of marimba bars gives the impression of legato at a particular tempo. In general, piano pieces in which the pedal serves a major role rarely work. Give special consideration to somewhat obscure pieces, or ones by slightly obscure composers; these can often make for intriguing adaptations and perhaps bring to light the work of an overlooked composer. If you wish to transcribe the work of a living composer, I suggest you ask their permission.

My ultimate goal with transcriptions is to bring something positive to a piece of music by bringing it to the marimba. It shows no disrespect to a composer or their work to present it through another prism—that is, on another instrument—if the intent of the music is still intact and, if in the new form, the piece presents a convincing vehicle for expression.

Transcriptions (vs. Adaptations vs. Arrangements)

I've been using the word "transcription," but one often hears the terms "adaptation" and "arrangement," too. One day, I looked them all up in a reputable music dictionary and found the definition for each of the three words was the other two! While this implies that they are simply interchangeable, I had the sense that perhaps in some circles they wouldn't (or shouldn't) be. I consulted the highly-regarded musician and composer Gunther Schuller for his opinion, which made perfect sense to me. Since that time, I have heard many others corroborate his view:

"Adaptation" is the preferred word if you have taken a piece of music that is written for one instrument (or group of instruments) and undertaken to play it on another instrument (or group of instruments). This could include, for instance, a guitar piece such as "Los Paraguas" by Federico Chueca, or a piano piece such as "For Susanna Kyle" by Leonard Bernstein (both of which are in Section IV), which were playable on marimba exactly as they were originally notated, making only the smallest modifications (which were made for this book). Or, it could include a case such as Debussy's "The snow is dancing," which I chose to recopy to make it look more "marimbistic." Even though I put some extra thought and work into this, I still didn't implement any major original ideas in order to bring this to the marimba. The same would be true even if I'd reduced a string quartet or orchestral score into a marimba solo or ensemble piece. So, whether or not you recopy the music, if you are only making minor changes to the original written notes, you are creating an "adaptation."

"Transcription" is used in a case in which the music was not previously written down. If you personally transcribed the music from listening to a recording (that is, wrote it down yourself, and that was the first time you saw it notated), then you made a transcription. This was the case for Michael Hedges' "Ragamuffin." I wrote it down from listening to a recording of his solo guitar version and, along the way, interpreted how certain guitar effects could be transferred to the marimba. Therefore, I transcribed *and* adapted that piece.

"Arrangement" is accurate in a case in which you have added significant original ideas to someone else's written music. An example might be if you took a lead sheet for a pop tune or jazz standard and, based on it, wrote out a solo marimba version with a rhythmic underpinning you invented, reharmonizations of some of the chords, and set it all within a structure you devised.

Be Yourself

In my teaching career, I have never created a syllabus of "must-learn" marimba pieces or come to expect my students to move through a predetermined progression of pieces of any kind. The reason for this is that so much marimba music is mediocre, and because I'd rather see every player build a personal repertoire of pieces he or she likes. I certainly make suggestions and try to encourage variety, but I also expect students to have their ears to the ground for ideas of their own. My aim is to continually emphasize personal expression. Hopefully, players' tastes will continually broaden in scope and their careers will lead them to taking on challenges that will lead to surprising discoveries. It's a journey, and it should be full of joy.

When I arrive at a marimba recital, I am excited to look at the program and see what treats may be in store. Especially given the limited repertoire available to marimbists, I am intrigued when I see that someone has dealt with the problem imaginatively. If the program entirely comprises marimba pieces I've heard before, or even adaptations I've heard before, I'm a bit disappointed. But if the programming is clearly original—perhaps including a new work, some transcriptions I've never heard of, a composition or adaptation by the performer *along with* some famous marimba pieces—then I'm full of anticipation. I know this could well be a special experience! I know, even before they play, that the performer is trying to say something personal through his or her choice of music and its progression through the upcoming event—which bodes well that the same may happen once I am "in the moment" of this performer's music-making.

I care most about listening to people who, I can tell, want to play with all their heart, and who are willing, if not desperate, to reveal something through their playing that can *only* be revealed through their music. The closer you feel to the music you play, the more likely this communication can happen.

How to Practice

Many practicing basics that will be of use to players of all levels are in Section I-L. How to Practice. This chapter expands on some of those ideas and introduces additional ones.

On Exercises

Many students have asked me to recommend good warm-up exercises. I always get the feeling they're hoping I have a set of miracle exercises up my sleeve that will instantaneously turn them into great players. My reply (and this book) is probably a disappointment to them. Generally, I don't endorse exercises (apart from my suggestion in Section I-L. How to Practice, that you can create exercises out of difficult passages you're learning, which I will expand on below).

Many people are drawn to exercises. People should play what they enjoy and, if you enjoy exercises, you should certainly include them in your practice sessions. I imagine the appeal is the physical work-out, as well as the fact that exercises are such straightforward measuring sticks; it's easy to tell if you've made progress if, at first, you can't play some tricky configuration and, after some work, you can.

To be honest, if I practiced exercises, I would probably have better technique. But I hate practicing exercises and (especially now that I'm approaching middle age) would much rather focus on the musical values I *do* care about. In my formative years, however, I practiced some that have proven very helpful. Among them were some two-mallet exercises taught me by Ian Finkel (including the Double-Sticking Exercise in Section III-B. Relationship of Sticking Choices to Phrasing) and all the scales. In general, since I can't bear to practice exercises myself, it wouldn't be fair to write a book and suggest that people do so.

My aversion to exercises is, in part, a revolt against the "percussion mindset." Many marimba players come to the instrument by way of percussion. Percussionists are probably more obsessed with exercises than any other group of instrumentalists. There are many good reasons for this. They need to have very a firmly-ingrained sense of time, very precise motor skills, and physical stamina. Most exercise-obsessed marimbists are usually also percussionists who practice the way they always practice. Of course, the marimba is a percussion instrument, can be played extremely rhythmically, and can require a lot of technical stamina. My personal preference, however, is to acknowledge its percussive qualities, but try to emphasize its lyrical ones.

When I first showed the studies I composed for Section II to some of my students, they obviously had difficulty hiding their disappointment. I think they were hoping they would finally get the "miracle exercises" they'd been waiting for. They didn't understand in what way they were "studies," since they didn't address building physical stamina or muscles. Yet, my students agreed that, to play them with attention to every detail—tempo, style, phrasing, dynamics, articulations, as well as with note accuracy and technical control—was quite difficult.

Practice Toward Your Goal

If your goal is to be a good marimbist and musician, you need to spend your time practicing everything that goes into that. My studies, for instance, hopefully provide the kind of mixture of challenges that arise in actual music. Every moment you practice, you should be concentrating on improving and refining your musical imagination and your ear for music. Our ears can lead us to make certain refinements and improvements in technique that basic technical exercises never will.

The specific way you distribute your time when you practice should correlate to your goals and priorities. If, for instance, you know you need to work on expression, it will not help you to accomplish your goal if you spend half of each practice session on technical warm-ups; you need to be playing pieces that hold the possibility for expression. If you are under enormous pressure to learn a piece in a short time, it's silly to spend half your practice time on warm-ups; spend it all on the piece! Under normal circumstances, you may: (1) be working on two contrasting solos, (2) need to practice parts for two ensemble pieces to which you've been assigned, (3) need general work on sight-reading, and (4) want to improve your one-handed rolls. In that case, each practice session should be divided among those particular goals, relative to your priorities.

Your practice sessions ought to be efficient. It's much more important to practice thoughtfully for a few hours than to play mindlessly for five or six hours just to meet a quota you may have in mind.

It's inefficient to practice pieces in "stages." Some people have the idea that they want to learn the notes first; then later, they will consider the dynamics, where the phrases are, what articulations there are, and finally, perhaps, memorize it. This makes no sense!

If a note is marked ***p***, but you ignore the ***p***, you are not playing the note accurately, so you have not learned it! When we learn a new piece, part of what we are doing is training our muscles how to move (frequently called "muscle memory"). In order to produce a beautiful sound, begin a phrase, or play with a certain articulation or dynamic, we use our muscles in particular ways. You need to be ingraining all of that right from the start.

Your musical imagination should also be eager and active, looking for a way into the music behind the notes, from the first moment you begin to look at a new piece. Every element of the notation is there to show you the architecture and parameters of the music, but the important stuff is usually inside; you have to discover it! This is where the music is!

Difficult Passages

In Section I-L. How to Practice, I introduced the idea of making a list of difficult passages in music you're learning and using them as a warm-up. An example of how I sometimes expand on difficult passages and create exercises from them can be seen in Section V in the chapter on Steven Mackey's "See Ya Thursday," under Performance Advice on Excerpt III.

Earlier in this chapter I said I would have better technique if I practiced exercises. "Technique" is a very general term. If I practiced flashy patterns of ascending and descending octaves and arpeggios, or repeatedly pounded out chords, I would certainly build muscles (which are part of technique) but, in terms of the specific performance techniques I would have learned, I would only be better at playing octaves, arpeggios, and repeated chords. If there existed a piece of music that called for those performance techniques, I'd be the woman for the job. But, the problem is that those patterns rarely appear in pieces of music.

If you really love playing exercises, I advise you to reconsider what exercises you practice and perhaps begin to relate them more to the difficult passages within music you're currently playing. Perhaps you can expand on them as I did with the example from "See Ya Thursday."

You might even keep a notebook of these. Such a journal could be a fascinating way to chart your technical development. If you and some friends agree to do this, you might even occasionally trade notebooks to check out some extra technical exercises—all of which sprang from actual music! (In so doing, you will also learn more about existing repertoire, and possibly gain ideas for music you would like to learn.)

Learn a Lot of Music

I mentioned that exercises can be a reassuring, straightforward measuring stick of your improvement. By comparison, when you have learned yet another piece, it may feel more difficult to tell whether your playing has generally improved. But it has! Even if the piece is not one you want to add to your official repertoire list, every piece of music you learn is like money in the bank. Every piece you play makes you a richer musician.

The technique that truly matters is that of flexibility as a musician. This can only be learned over time, through playing many pieces of music, having many musical experiences, and having contact with many musicians. There are no miraculous ways to learn this in a hurry. The more music you have played, the deeper the pool of resources from which you can draw in order to play with more imagination, more sensitivity, and more intelligence, which will create more beautiful music.

Other Practice Guidelines

1. Visualization, in practicing and performing, is extremely important. You must see in your mind's eye what notes you need to play next, and hear in your imagination how you want to play them, *before* you get to them. This can very positively impact note accuracy.
2. You can be your own best teacher by listening to yourself. It's extremely valuable to record yourself and listen back objectively.
3. If you are lucky enough to consistently make mistakes in the same spot (as opposed to different mistakes every time through a passage or piece), really study what you are doing wrong. Zero in on a habitual wrong note and study what it sounds like (in context) when you play it on purpose. This helps your ear be more finely tuned to catching the wrong note. Then, when you practice with the correct note, your hands, and your imagination, will be more keenly focused on the correct target.
4. When you are learning chorales or pieces with complicated harmonies (especially ones in the low register of the marimba), it can be very helpful to play them on the piano where they will sound more homogenous (or even on the marimba, played an octave higher). Marimba overtones play funny tricks. You'll be able to render more balanced chords if you can hear them more clearly in your mind.
5. Finally, I will reiterate one idea I have touched on several times, which is the single most important thing to think about as you play. Always concentrate on the sound you are producing—not *how* you are producing it. Difficult passages are always easier if you focus on how you want them to sound, rather than the specific technical issues of playing them.

Miscellaneous Thoughts

1. Sometimes I think memorization is overrated. It does look nice to see marimbists play without a music stand in front of them to block the view. For my own performing (this is admittedly perhaps a bit crazy), I like the statement the music stand makes that I am, in fact, playing notated music and actively referring to what the composer wanted to tell me. I am also a visual person who is ever-anxious to see more deeply into a piece—for more ideas about how to play it better—and it's much easier for me to make these kinds of discoveries when I am looking at the notes. Furthermore, much of the type of playing I love most is very spread out across a five-octave instrument. The best way to approach this physically is to feel "centered" and to reach to the sides by feel; my music keeps me centered.
2. There is some debate over the wisdom of allowing students to learn a piece of music that is "over their head." My position is that, within reason, I don't like to squelch anyone's enthusiasm. There are cases in which I can see that a piece is so far over someone's head that there will be nothing to be gained from the person trying it, so I do discourage them. In other cases, however, students are able to do a pretty good job with a piece that is, on many levels, too difficult for them, and the attempt can help their playing take a leap. As long as they understand the gaps they still need to fill in, no harm is done. Plus, if they return to that piece later when they are better equipped to handle it, they may make some interesting discoveries. Much can be gained by returning to a piece you worked on at an earlier time.
3. A frequent topic of consideration for marimbists is the problem of wrong notes. It is terribly difficult to play the marimba without hitting some wrong notes, which do detract from a performance. No one wants to hit them! We can only try our best not to and, beyond that, focus on a more important aspect of performing: playing

the music. If you are deeply inside "playing the music" of a piece, and you clearly have your listeners with you on that "magic carpet ride," no one is going to mind if there's a mistake or two; they will be enjoying the ride too much!

It's unusual for most performers to finish a performance and feel absolutely great about it. There are almost always things we wish had gone better. This is why we push ourselves to strive for better each *next* time. I think we need to be able to be a bit gentle with ourselves, too. Usually, we're comparing ourselves to the very best we know we can play a piece; it usually only goes *that* well one out of ten times we play it, but we are still hard on ourselves when that one time didn't happen in a particular performance situation. The important thing is the general level at which you play. It will include some mistakes, because we are all human. We need to strive for our best to be better, but also for our "average" to be very good!

Philosophies on Interpretation

Every note in a piece of music has a purpose. It is leading somewhere, or leading away from somewhere. It should have a particular character, or be part of a group of notes with a particular character. It should be played at a particular dynamic and with a certain feeling because of the aforementioned considerations. If someone stopped you in the middle of playing a piece and said, "*That* note; tell me about *that* one!," you should be able to give it a context.

A good way to begin thinking more about these types of things is through dynamics. Every dynamic, along with the notes it applies to, should give you some clues about a feeling inherent in the music that you might amplify in some way. When you see ***p***, it can suggest many things, depending on its context: delicate, sweet, innocent, playful, giggling, gentle, calm, whispery, distant, uncertain, mysterious, sinister, or a hundred other adjectives related to feelings. A great exercise is to associate an adjective to every dynamic in a piece of music, so that you are doing more than playing the dynamics; you are trying to play *feelings*.

The way your imagination works to make decisions such as these is all yours! This can be one of the first steps in forming an interpretation of a piece. This explains one of the wonders of music: that different people can play the same piece of music well and yet each sound completely different!

Take into account other features of a piece such as the use of recurring themes or motives, important harmonic movement, or the overall structure. Sometimes you can invent some type of story line that exists for you within a piece. Other times, you might have strong images at certain points in a piece. A starting point could involve imagining what type of person a piece would be! Would it be male or female? How old? How would he or she dress? In what colors? What type of personality would this person have? What types of things would this person like to do?

Imagery such as this helps many people connect more deeply to what they're playing. The audience will rarely, if ever, "receive" the same imagery you focus on, yet I believe that the act of focusing on it increases a performer's chances of making the music come across potently.

Sometimes we have to play music we don't like. I feel strongly that this builds character! Using some of these imagery associations can be very helpful in these instances. In order to play a piece you don't like and play it well, you need to discover *something* you can bring to it. Oftentimes, there is some satisfaction to be gained from rendering a piece with a lot of character; that is, making the most you can with what is there. Occasionally, once you've made this kind of effort with a piece, it even turns out that you *do* like it.

In interpreting a piece, my general outlook is that I want to see how much I can adhere to the composer's directives (known through elements of notation) and also how much I can bring to it from my own imagination. I want to find a balance in which I have made the music personal for me and also made the composer's notes come to life. Performers are perfectly capable of pleasantly surprising composers. We can make their music sound even better than they had imagined. The reason is that it's almost impossible for a composer to envision that magical element of "life" performers can bring to a piece once our imaginations catch fire.

Play From Your Heart

If your goal is to play the marimba artistically, to have a hand in bringing the marimba into more respected prominence in the concert music world or into further enjoyment within your community, you will have a much greater chance at success if you are the best musician you can be. The key is playing music deeply and expressively. Being able to touch someone is a far greater power than being able to "wow" them with your technique. "Flashy," technical playing—only for the sake of being flashy—promises only to rekindle or perpetuate the marimba as a vaudeville and novelty instrument (as it was in the 1920s to 40s) which, in my view, would be a shame. The future of the marimba rests in the hands of those who elevate the marimba's artistic stature by playing from their hearts.

Section Four 18 Intermediate-to-Advanced Adapted Solos

1. **"Climbing Mountain"** by Mason Daring (Low-F Marimba)
2. **"Maybe"** by Jean Hasse (5-Octave Marimba)
3. **"Bow Bells"** by Jean Hasse (Low-A Marimba)
4. **"Allegro"** by Anonymous (Low-A or 5-Octave Marimba)
5. **"Sarabande"** by George Frederick Handel (Low-A or 5-Octave Marimba)
6. **"Allegretto"** by Anonymous (Low-A or Low-E Marimba)
7. **"Solfeggietto"** by Carl Philipp Emanuel Bach (Low-F or 5-Octave Marimba)
8. **"Danses de travers No. 1"** by Erik Satie (Low-A or 5-Octave Marimba)
9. **"The snow is dancing"** by Claude Debussy (Low-A or 5-Octave Marimba)
10. **"For Susanna Kyle"** by Leonard Bernstein (5-Octave Marimba)
11. **"Prélude, Op. 28, Nº 15"** by Frédéric Chopin (5-Octave Marimba)
12. **"Los Paraguas"** by Federico Chueca (Low-A or 5-Octave Marimba)
13. **"Bagatelle Nº 4, Op. 126"** by Ludwig van Beethoven (5-Octave Marimba)
14. **"Morning Glory"** by Duke Ellington (5-Octave Marimba)
15. **"Quincy"** by David Friedman (5-Octave Marimba)
16. **"Wallflower"** by Dan Trueman (Low-F Marimba)
17. **"A La Orilla de un Palmar"** (Traditional Mexican) (5-Octave Marimba)
18. **"Ragamuffin"** by Michael Hedges (5-Octave Marimba)

Climbing Mountain

(1997)

"Climbing Mountain" was composed for the soundtrack of John Sayles' 1998 film *Men With Guns (Hombres Armados)*. It's the only piece in this section of the book that was conceived to be played on marimba. My recording for the soundtrack is available on Rykodisc (CD #10437).

Maybe

from *Pocket Pieces for Piano, Book I* (1998)

"Maybe" was recorded by Jean Hasse on the CD *Kinkh* (Visible Music VM-CD 101). (No changes were made to the original except for the removal of pedaling indications.) Try to give the impression through the kind of stroke you use that where dotted-quarters, half notes, and dotted-halves are used, you are playing longer notes (than eighths) without rolling.

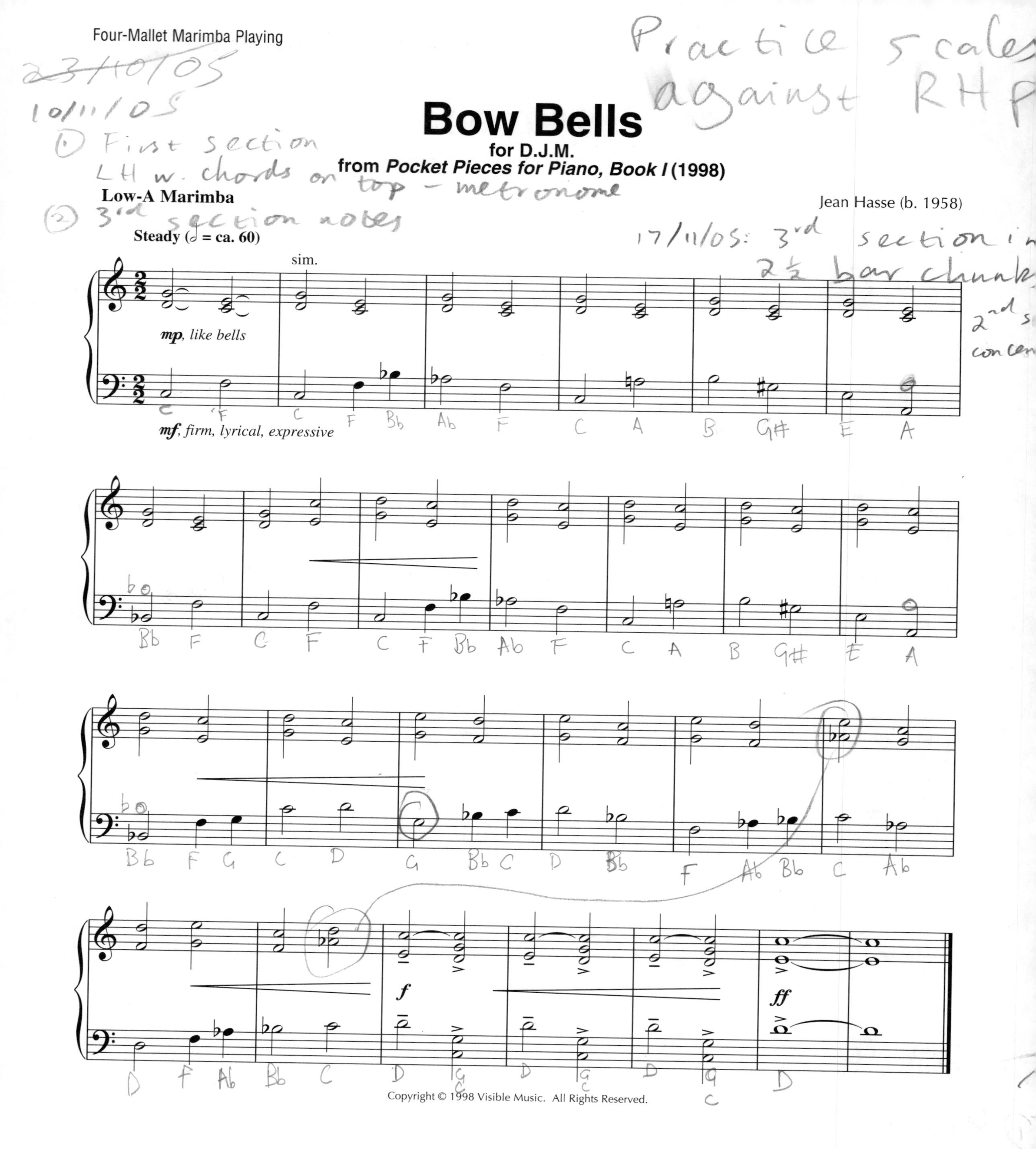

"Bow Bells" was recorded by Jean Hasse on the CD *Kinkh* (Visible Music VM-CD 101). (No changes were made to the original except for the removal of pedaling indications.) I suggest practicing this piece without rolls to work on a full, rich tone and playing well-balanced chords, keeping in mind the composer's indication for the left hand to be stronger than the right. Also, make the voice-leading of the moving lines clear.

15/12/05

Allegro

No. 2 from *Six Lute Pieces of the Renaissance*

Anonymous
Adapt. Nancy Zeltsman

Like guitar music, lute music sounds an octave lower than it is notated, so marimbists may play the piece one octave lower than written (if you have a 5-octave instrument).

In early and Baroque-period music, trills customarily begin on the upper neighbor note in the key. Therefore, the first trill would be between G and F-sharp; the second trill would be between D and C-sharp. I suggest playing both trills one-handed, with mallet 3 playing the upper note and mallet 4 playing the lower note (in the center beating spot).

Brackets indicate that you could play the lowest note (D) as a grace note to the double-stop F-sharp/D's. I suggest playing the grace note and F-sharp with the left hand. (This is suggested as an alternative to sounding the three notes of the chord together, which requires a rather awkward wrist twist to play top F-sharp/D in the right hand. However, you could opt to play the three notes simultaneously.)

In the five-note chord (following the first repeat) it's fine to omit the B in parentheses. If you don't omit it, a recommended sticking, from the bottom up (which is how you would ripple) is 1, 2, 3, 2, 4.

Most dynamics are left up to the performer. Recommended tempo is approximately quarter note = 126–144.

→ 15/12/05

1) Practice LH melody: LH mel + high chords
LH mel + low chords without break

2) Learn 3rd section in 2 bar phrases.
Work from the end backwards

3) Practice final chords.

Sarabande

George Frederick Handel (1685–1759)
Transcribed for guitar by Frantz Casseus
Edited for marimba by Nancy Zeltsman

Originally published in the collection *World's Favorite Selected Masterpieces for Classic Guitar* (World's Favorite Series No. 56)

Since guitar music sounds an octave lower than it is notated, marimbists may play the piece one octave lower than written (if you have a 5-octave instrument). Brackets indicate that you should play the lowest note as a grace note before the main chord. Dynamics are left up to the performer. Recommended tempo is approximately half note = 60. (It could work to play the variations at slightly different tempos.) I suggest playing this piece without rolls. Use it to practice playing very full, rich, ringing chords.

Allegretto

No. 3 from *Three Fifteenth Century Songs*

Anonymous
Transcibed for guitar by Frantz Casseus
Edited for marimba by Nancy Zeltsman

Low-A or Low-E Marimba

Originally published in the collection *World's Favorite Selected Masterpieces for Classic Guitar* (World's Favorite Series No. 56)

Since guitar music sounds an octave lower than it is notated, marimbists may play the piece one octave lower than written (if you have a low-E instrument). (Personally, I prefer this piece in the written register.) Dynamics are left up to the performer.

Solfeggietto

originally for piano

Carl Philipp Emanuel Bach (1714–1788)
Adapt. Nancy Zeltsman

Low-F or 5-Octave Marimba

(a) Play an octave: the lowest two of these notes available on your marimba.

Danses de travers No. 1

from *Pièces Froides* for piano

à Madame J. Écorcheville

Low-A or 5-Octave Marimba

Erik Satie (1866–1925)

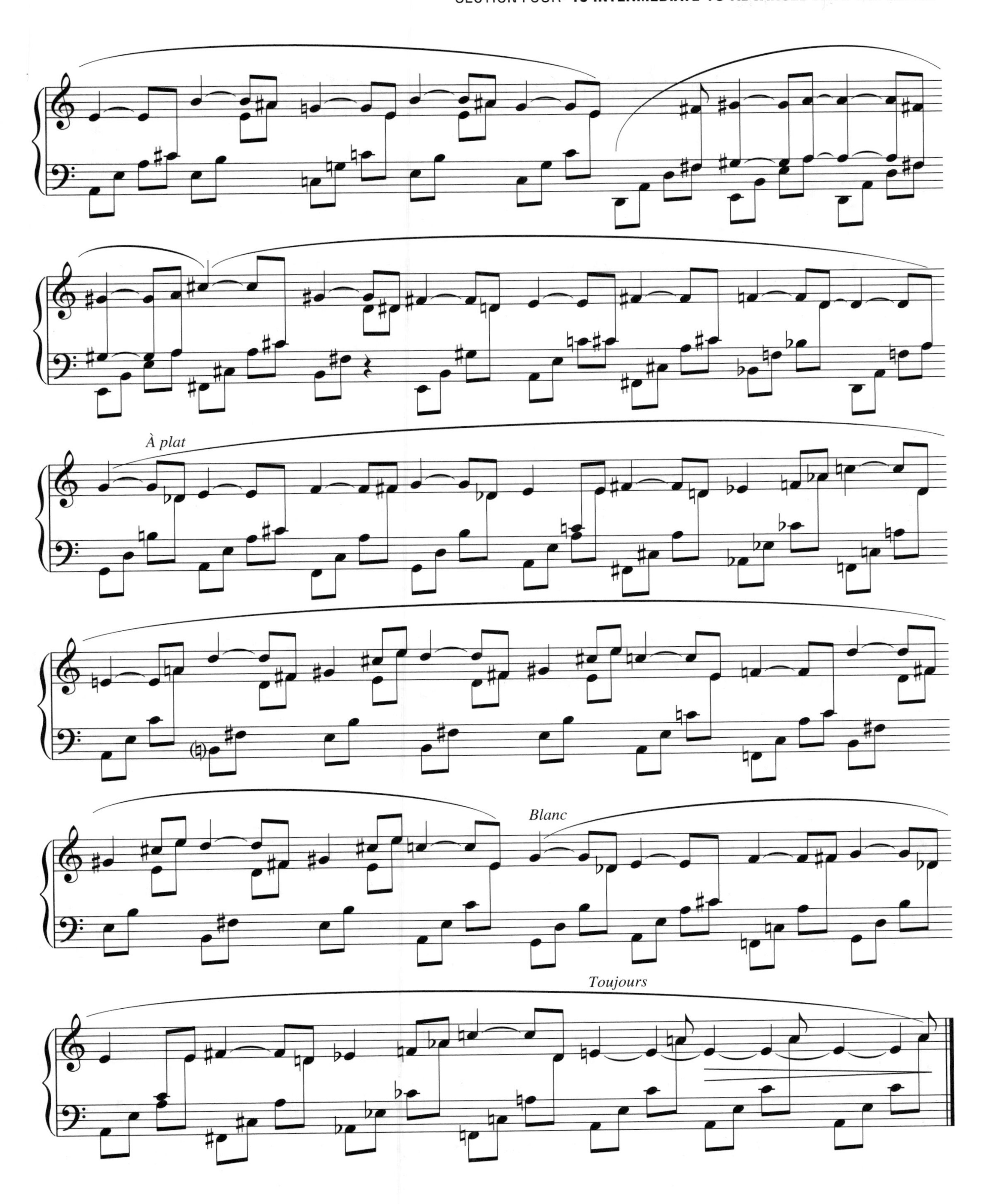

This piece can be played 8va if you do not have a 5-octave (low-C) marimba. Dynamics are left up to the performer. Recommended tempo is quarter note = ca. 144

The snow is dancing

IV. from *Children's Corner* for piano (1908)

Claude Debussy (1862–1918)
Adapt. Nancy Zeltsman

Opt.: staccatos = quasi dead strokes

più
p
mp
più
p
mp
4
gently and sadly
3
4
2 2 2
più p
4
pp
2

*On a five-octave, omit L.H. on beat 3 and play both hands 8vb (one octave lower) for the next four measures (minus the last two 𝅘𝅥𝅮s).

with motion
f
f
f
f
f
p
più p
pp
più
p

with motion
più p
pp
più
p

sempre pp
pp
ppp
pp
pp
without slowing

For Susanna Kyle

(born July 24, 1949)
V. from *Five Anniversaries* for piano (1949)

Leonard Bernstein (1918–1990)

*Play bottom system chord as a grace note to the E. Roll all but the A.

"For Susanna Kyle" was recorded by Nancy Zeltsman on the CD *See Ya Thursday* (Equilibrium EQ29). (No changes were made to the original except for the addition of rolls.)

Prélude

Op. 28, No. 15
originally for piano (c. 1837)

5-Octave Marimba

Frédéric Chopin (1810–1849)
Adapt. Nancy Zeltsman

7
1st time: sotto voce / 2nd time: p
4 4 3
3
p cresc.
(cresc.)
ff
1.
2.
3 3
2 dim.
sf dim.
p

p
f
p
dim. e rit.
p
smorzando
10
slentando
f
p
pp
riten.

Los Paraguas

(The Umbrellas)

Low-A or 5-Octave Marimba

Federico Chueca (1846–1908)
Transcribed for guitar by Francisco Tárrega
Adapt. Nancy Zeltsman

sim.
rapido, con enegia
mp/p
mp
p
1.
2.

cresc.
4 →
mf
sim.
mp
p
sim.
molto cresc.
f
4 3 3 3 4
mf

This piece could be played in the octave in which it is written, but sounds much better an octave lower (as it would sound on the guitar). Recommended tempo is quarter note = ca.126–138. I like to be quite flexible with the tempo as long as a dance-like quality is preserved. "Los Paraguas" was recorded by Nancy Zeltsman on the CD *See Ya Thursday* (Equilibrium EQ29).

Bagatelle No. 4

from *Six Bagatelles*, Op. 126 (1824) for pianoforte

Ludwig van Beethoven (1770–1827)
Adapt. Nancy Zeltsman

3
R
L
R
f
p
p
4
3
4
R
L
L
R
L
R
sempre p
R
L
R
f
L
R
L
2
1
sf
sf
sf
sf
sf
sf

3
R
L
R
f
p
4
3
4
p
R
L
L
R
L
R
sempre p
f
L
R
L
R
L
R
2
1
sf
sf
sf
sf
sf
sf

To Coda
(last time)
1.
2.
sf
sf
p
p
p
cresc.
pp
pp
2
cresc.
p
p
cresc.

"Bagatelle N° 4" was recorded by Nancy Zeltsman on the CD *See Ya Thursday* (Equilibrium EQ29).

Morning Glory

originally for piano

"Morning Glory" was recorded by Nancy Zeltsman on the CD *See Ya Thursday* (Equilibrium EQ29).

Quincy

(1999)

from *Beyond Dreams: Piano Music for Musicians*

David Friedman (b. 1944)
Adapt. Nancy Zeltsman

19
To Coda
23
mf
dim.
mp
27
C
(poco)
31
mf
34

38
p sub. cresc.
f
dim. poco a poco
43
D
mp
47
mf
51
D.S. al Coda
CODA
3
55
3
p
p

Wallflower

Low-F Marimba
Dan Trueman (b. 1968)
Adapt. Nancy Zeltsman
♩ = 138
mf
sim.
mp
mf
mp
mf
mp
sim.
mp
mf
*× = Optional: play with head and shaft of mallet

21
mp
(mp)
25
sim.
29
33
cresc.
f
37
(all R.H. except where indicated)
41

45
dim.
poco a poco
49
p
mp
53
p
57
mf
60
p
mp
64
4 2

68
cresc. poco a poco
72
76
f
80
84
88
p sub.
(p)

92
cresc.
96
rhythmically
100
mf
dim.
p
sim.
104
108
cresc. poco a poco
112
116

120
f
124
127
131
135
dim.
139
f sub.

"Wallflower" was originally composed for 6-string electric fiddle. It was recorded by Dan Trueman on the CD *Trollstilt* (Azalea City Recordings ACCD 2004).

A La Orilla de un Palmar

(c. 1938)
(In the Grove Among the Palms)

Traditional Mexican
English lyric by Paul Olga
Arranged by Ricardo Romero
Adapt. Nancy Zeltsman

5-Octave Marimba

poco rit.
1.
a tempo
mf
2.
a tempo
mp

Originally for voice/piano. I like to use uncovered latex rubber-headed mallets for this piece: Encore 25LB for mallet 1, plus three Encore 24LB mallets. Recommended tempo is quarter note = ca.84. (I like to be quite flexible with the tempo.) "A La Orilla de un Palmar" was recorded by Nancy Zeltsman on the CD *See Ya Thursday* (Equilibrium EQ29).

Lyrics:

In the grove among the palms, I once saw a maiden roaming,
Lips were little coral gems, Eyes were stars at twilight's gloaming.
When I asked the pretty maid The reason for all her roaming,
She replied "Because I'm all alone, And live among the palms.

I have no father, I never have known a mother,
No dear companion, ever offered me his hand,
And I wander by myself 'Mongst all the palms of this lonely land,
Like the little lonely waves that roll and beat upon the strand."

Ragamuffin

5-Octave Marimba

Michael Hedges (1953–1997)
Transcribed and adapted by Nancy Zeltsman

Notes in parentheses should be ghosted. Play staccatos as dead strokes.
*On repeats, previous eighth note is tied over; omit beat 1.
**On D.C./2nd time, add G on top of B and D on beat 3.
On final D.C. (before coda), add D above on beat 2-&, and A above on beat 3.

13
(click mallet handles)
(no roll)
ff
(Play with handle
and mallet head)
16
(fast roll)
(fast roll)
19
22
(fast roll)
(handle & head)
gliss.
mf sub.
gliss.
cresc.
gliss.
(On D.C. play low C instead on beat 1-&)
(2nd time: handle & head)
25
1st time: D.C. (take repeat)
2nd time: D.C. al Coda
f
mp sub.
(2nd time: handle & head)
CODA
cantabile
(mp)

(click handle on bar)
gliss.
(click handle on bar)
gliss.
(click handle on bar)

"Ragamuffin" was originally recorded on guitar by Michael Hedges on his album *Aerial Boundaries* (Windham Hill 1032). Administered by Imaginary Road Music (BMI). Nancy Zeltsman's transcription of the piece for marimba is recorded on her CD *Woodcuts* (GM Recordings GM2043CD).

Section Five Advanced Solos and Chamber Music: Excerpts and Commentary

SOLOS

Paul Lansky
Photo by Betty Freeman

Three Moves for Marimba (1998)
for solo marimba

by Paul Lansky (b. 1944)

Errata

These corrections apply to the original published music. The excerpts used in this book have been corrected.

- "Hop(2)," m. 17: Beat 4, third sixteenth note should be F-natural (on bottom staff).
- "Hop(2)," m. 18: Beat 4 should be F-natural (on top staff). Beat 4, third sixteenth note should be F-natural (on bottom staff).
- "Hop(2)," m. 22: Beat 4, second sixteenth note should be E-natural (on bottom staff).
- "Hop(2)," m. 41: Beat 3, fourth sixteenth note should have a cautionary G-natural (on top staff, since G-flat was just played in the left hand).
- "Hop(2)," m. 49: Sticking for fourth sixteenth note should be 1 (not 4).
- "Slide," m. 119: Seventh sixteenth note should have a cautionary F-sharp (on bottom staff, since F-natural was just played in the right hand).
- "Slide," m. 135: Beat 2, second sixteenth note should be C-sharp (on top staff).
- "Slide," m. 139: Third sixteenth note double-stop should be D-flat and E-flat.
- "Slide," m. 141: Fifth sixteenth note should be B-flat.
- "Slide," m. 158: Beat 3, D and F (on bottom staff) should be natural (despite sharped D and F on top system, previous beat).

General Information/Advice:

"Three Moves" sprang from my begging Paul Lansky to write a marimba solo based on the final section of his violin/marimba duo "Hop" (composed for Marimolin in 1993). The first eleven measures of that section (mm. 112–122) are identical to the opening eleven measures of "Hop(2)," the first movement of "Three Moves." (In "Hop," the marimba plays alone for the first three measures, then the violin joins in, playing a soft counterline in half notes that all fall on beats two and four until the final two bars when the violin plays on main beats.) After those first eleven bars, the material in "Hop(2)" develops rather differently from the remainder of "Hop."

The "three moves" are separate movements titled "Hop(2)," "Turn," and "Slide." The titles describe physical movements or gestures while slyly giving clues to the mood of each piece. For Lansky, they captured something about the quirky moves marimbists make to navigate the instrument.

"Hop(2)," marked "Find a groove," is pretty funky. I frequently practice this movement with a metronome clicking on the "ands" of every beat. It helps me to sink into the groove in a relaxed way, which I hope is still there when the metronome is turned off. The subdivisions should be very even, with perhaps a tiny sense of settling at the cadences of the first four sections (which end with a quarter-note rest on beat 4). To have a really funky feel, it helps to sing (that is, some sort of vocalized approximation) the syncopated phrases to see which parts of them you can accentuate, and which you might "ghost" a bit, to make them more groovy.

The second movement, "Turn," is marked "Assertively, proudly." On Lansky's first draft it was marked, "Like a Union song." To me, that is a great image for playing this movement. I envision a group of men singing their Union or company song together, feeling pride in it, enjoying the familiarity of the song, yet perhaps also feeling a little self-conscious about being a group of men enjoying the song. Therefore, I imagine they are singing a little stiffly, not wanting to give away the sentimentality they might truly feel.

In playing this piece at a fairly steady tempo, in one beat to a bar (like a huge, slow-swinging pendulum), but with a deep subdivisions in three, there is also a dichotomy of time-feel. The mood is very soulful, but it seems like I ought not give in to the depth of emotion—as if there is some protocol for remaining a bit stiff or aloof.

"Slide," the final movement, is marked "Steadily, project the meters." Lansky wants emphasis on each downbeat and, secondarily, the first notes of beamed rhythmic groupings, so that the meters are always clear. Emphasis on phrase beginnings should be subordinate to the latter. (If you have a metronome that subdivides into monotone-pitched triplets, set it to between quarter = 105–115 for a steady stream of clicks to the sixteenth notes at the tempos indicated. Of course, you could begin on a lower setting.) In the bigger picture, it is important to present the movement with a convincing arc—through the progression of dynamics and moods—in order for it to provide a solid close to "Three Moves" as a whole.

The pieces were conceived as a set and, generally, should not be played individually in concert (nor should two movements be played as a pair). In a competition, audition or jury setting, in which time is limited, it would be fine to play only one movement.

The first and third movements are extremely difficult. (Despite my openness to occasionally tackling a piece that is "over your head," this one is not a good candidate. I recommend that you play several advanced pieces before this one.) There isn't a bar that, taken by itself, isn't playable, but the relentless stream of difficult bars adds up to being quite daunting. It helps me to try to think ahead and very keenly visualize what moves are coming. This is helpful in all playing, but essential in "Three Moves."

Lansky was pretty open-minded about mallet choices and would probably be happy with a number of possibilities. For "Hop(2)," I experimented a lot and ultimately found I liked fairly soft mallets. In weighing the pros and cons of soft mallets, the "cons" are that they invite more "woo-woo" (resonance-hum). Given the expanse of the instrument covered through the use of many wide intervals (which give the resonance of each tone plenty of time and space to blossom), the sonorities are extremely rich. For me, the "pros" of choosing soft mallets are that the fundamental pitches are much clearer, particularly in the bass. While harder mallets maintain clarity, I began to find the high overtones they produced quite grating. The compromise I arrived at was Encore NZ7, 4, 3, 2.

Mallet choices in "Turn" are not so difficult, as most of the piece lies in the middle register. However, you need to keep a fairly soft mallet for the bass notes that arise. I ultimately decided on something like NZ6, 4, 2, 2. (Worn-out NZ3s would also be okay in the right hand, but I prefer the top notes to have a little bit of "bite.")

For "Slide" you need more definition than in the first movement because the notes go by so much faster. There are some high passages that can be beautifully crystalline with fairly hard mallets but lackluster with softer ones. I think you also need a soft-enough mallet in the 1 position that you can really dig into the bass notes without fear of damaging the bars. I use NZ5, 3, 2, 2.

Excerpt I: "Hop(2)," mm. 1–11

Performance Advice on Excerpt I

It's tricky to get into the groove right off the bat and, beyond that, establish the groove's "vibe"! This piece is very "hip" in its understatedness. (It's interesting to consider that, in most cases, it takes a lot of work to be understated.) The bass line (marked with tenutos) accentuates this. There is a distinct bluesy quality to this movement created by the frequent use of major and minor thirds in close succession. (For example, m. 1, beat 2, has both an E-flat and E-natural in the key of C; m. 2, beat 4, has both a D-flat and D-natural in the key of B-flat, etc.) There is an elusive melody line throughout that seems to dangle from the rich harmonies, inner voice leadings, and disjunct pitch configurations. Each performer needs to discover a melodic thread for himself or herself.

Excerpt II: "Hop(2)," mm. 39–41

Performance Advice on Excerpt II

The nearly continual fourths (and thirds) in the right hand are unusual. Maintaining good beating spots and, therefore, consistently good tone quality (throughout this section and the movement) requires tremendous clarity and concentration.

Excerpt III: "Hop(2)," mm. 59–end

Performance Advice on Excerpt III

Here, the challenging shifts between "white" and "black" notes continue. Keeping your mallets low can help note accuracy. I also try to minimize movement by aiming for edge beating spots on the "black" notes throughout (with the exception of the low B-flats and D-flats in m. 60, and the A-flat octave within the first beat of m. 62).

Excerpt IV: "Turn," mm. 1–20

Performance Advice on Excerpt IV

To me, the nature of the opening theme is quite introspective. Given that, the *mf* feels uncomfortably strident to me. I chalk that up to being another of the intentional ironies, and I do try to get quite a full sound at the beginning. (It's a bit of a relief when I get to play that theme more quietly and sensitively beginning in m. 56.) Note that the melody is in the alto voice. (The melody switches to the soprano voice in m. 21.) Try to find a tempo that isn't ploddy; there should be a sense of dignity but also of some forward motion. However, Lansky doesn't like the movement to be played any faster than dotted-quarter note = 58. If anything, a tad under that is preferable. It should not feel rushed.

Note that Lansky specifies that the rolls should be "gentle." He liked when I did the type of rolls I describe in Section III-C. Refining Rolls as trying to emulate a piano's sustain. I strike the chord at the appropriate dynamic level and then immediately drop back the dynamic level quite a bit; I can almost camouflage the fact that I'm rolling within the resonance of the initial attack.

Excerpt V: "Turn," mm. 76–103

Performance Advice on Excerpt V

The real challenge of "Turn" lies in consistently balancing the chords well—with the alto or soprano voice in the lead—and playing them all without flamming. Try to prepare to play every chord before you do. Somehow the challenge of playing without flams seems pronounced in passages like mm. 76–88 when there are so many dotted-quarter notes, but here you also have more time to prepare to play.

At letter C, I suggest trying to play with extremely heavy, slow strokes to get the broadest possible tone. (Be especially careful to prepare to play the last eighth-note chord in m. 121 in order to be convincing that the E-sharp is intentional.)

Excerpt VI: "Slide," mm. 28–46 (downbeat)

Performance Advice on Excerpt VI

This is another tricky spot in which, like Excerpt III, I mostly play on the edges of the "black" notes. I go to the centers for the D-flat/E-flat double-stops beginning in m. 33 and bass notes beginning in m. 34. (It's a small point, but in the left hand of m. 31, I now use a different sticking, 2, 2, 2, 2, 1, than appeared in the first edition of the score.)

Excerpt VII: "Slide," mm. 73–87

Performance Advice on Excerpt VII

The main difficulty in this section lies in the contrapuntal lines, each of which is played by one mallet (in mm. 73 and 74, and mm. 77–79). The trick to this technique is keeping your mallet heads low and using a very clearly directed stroke. Try to prepare as early as possible to play the double-stop arrival points in mm. 74–76, in order to find ideal beating spots and produce a clear tone. Measure 82 (letter C) marks the return of the opening theme of the movement. I try to make it recognizable by doing a slight crescendo into this bar (even though one is not marked) and bringing out the "swoopy" bar-long phrasings (which contrast the long lines of the preceding bars). Again, I mostly play on the edges of the "black" notes, except for possibly the left hand's B-flat in m. 75, and the bass notes of each grouping in mm. 80–87.

Excerpt VIII: "Slide," mm. 129–146

Performance Advice on Excerpt VIII

The beginning of this passage, of course, harkens back to the opening of the movement. Try to make that clear by playing it with a similar shaping and generous tone as you did at the opening, but in a manner appropriate for this register. Emphasize the descending line in the left hand in mm. 133–135 (which is also nice to bring out in mm. 121–124). In mm. 135–138, balance your hands carefully to give the impression of continuous double-stops (despite the occasional single note).

"Three Moves for Marimba" was recorded by Nancy Zeltsman on the CD *See Ya Thursday* (Equilibrium EQ29).

Steven Mackey
Photo by Betty Freeman

See Ya Thursday (1993)
for solo marimba

by Steven Mackey (b. 1956)

Errata

These corrections apply to the original published music. The excerpts used in this book have been corrected.

- Mallet suggestion: Steve liked the combination of Encore NZ7,4,2,1 (from left to right), which I used when I first played the piece, and recommended it in the score. Since then, I have come to feel (and have convinced Steve) that those right-hand mallets are a bit hard. I now prefer to use an NZ3 and NZ2 in the mallet 3 and 4 positions, respectively—ideally ones that are a bit broken in.
- m. 139 etc.: I recommend using mallet 2 on the left-hand B (as well as the E), and reserving mallet 1 for the bass notes only.
- m. 143: Add a 5/8 time signature.
- m. 147: Third eighth note should be G-sharp. (Then, the sharp on the last G eighth note is redundant.)
- m. 151: Third note should be F-sharp.
- m. 216: Time signature should be 7/8 (not 6/8).
- m. 247: Move "allargando molto" one measure later (to m. 248). Over the last three eighth notes of m. 247 (that is, the E's) add "poco accel."
- m. 271: Add a 3/4 time signature (and also at the end of m. 270).
- m. 350: The E dotted-half note should be E-flat.

General Information/Advice

The main objective behind this piece is to project the essence of storytelling. The title was tacked on after Steve finished composing the piece and refers to a particular story between us. However, it is perfectly plausible and acceptable for people to relate the piece to almost *any* story.

It's an unusual marimba piece and its challenges are atypical. Whereas most difficult marimba music has lots of notes, the notes in "See Ya Thursday" are relatively sparse. They often reveal the natural length of resonance/decay of marimba notes (while in faster pieces, the attention is mainly on each note's attack). Its demands lie in having an artistic conception, shaping the twelve-and-a-half-minute continuous piece so that it makes sense as one complete arc (or story), giving the utmost attention to quality of tone, and being extremely note-accurate. The relatively thin texture means that each note is critical to the harmony. The piece also benefits from a certain physical grace, since so much of the work embraces large expanses of the keyboard.

There are several primary ideas and motives throughout the piece:

1. The first is the idea of "breakdowns." This is seen in the opening line of the piece, in which the roll temporarily becomes quite spastic (see below), as well as the rest of Excerpt I. There is a tinge of the breakdown idea in the octave groupings in mm. 89–108 and the slight freedom of m. 111 and m. 114, but the next real breakdown area is what I refer to as the "irregular raindrops" section, which lasts for most of page 5. There's a brief hint of breakdown in the tempo shifts in mm. 247 and 248, which lead into the last main breakdown section—the most rhythmically intricate—the "Halting, nervous" Thelonious Monk-inspired section from mm. 249–270. From mm. 271–284, the thirty-second-note interjections are reminders of the opening of the piece, and expand on the octaves that have popped up occasionally. I suppose the gradual accelerandi and new-tempo plateaus from mm. 312–357 could possibly be viewed as a controlled breakdown in reverse!
2. The second important idea is the sense of suspended time achieved through the repeating motive comprising a bass note phrased to a tenor-register note—usually paced in a calm, gentle rhythm—which is first really seen in m. 13: the low D to A-flat. Steve refers to this as the "oom-pah." (By "suspended time" I am referring to the way this oom-pah motive gives the whole piece an underlying sense of slow and deliberate pacing, even when combined with faster ornamentation, as in m. 121.) It continues for the rest of page 2 and finally resolves to low C and G in mm. 39 and 40, nearing the end of the first big phrase of the piece. That motive continues with the low E to G-sharp in mm. 43 and 44, and so on. You should imagine a phrase mark drawn between every such bass and tenor note throughout the piece. Sink into each bass note (with a slow downstroke) and imagine the resonance gracefully connecting through to the tenor note, which should be played more lightly.
3. Space. There is lots of space in the piece: mm. 34, 42, 58–61, 76, 83–95, etc. Count accurately, but be relaxed and breathe in these spots. In fact, breathing is very important throughout the piece, so it feels like you have internalized the contours and metabolism of every gesture and phrase. (You are telling a story with which you are very familiar and which really matters to you.) It is important to feel comfortable in the spaces. (They create suspense and show confidence in your story.)
4. Registral separation. The pitches are often spread into distinctly separate regions of the keyboard. Besides the bass-to-tenor-note phrases (item 2 above), much of the piece explores the marimba's low, middle, and high registers simultaneously (first heard in mm. 26–41). This feature in probably enhanced by seeing the piece performed live.

To me, "See Ya Thursday" invites enormous imagination from the performer. There are many different characters and flavors in the piece. It demands that you deal with it at its own pace. So, my goal when I perform it is to savor every bit of the time it takes to play it, and to try to weave together all the colors and attitudes hidden in the notes with as much attention to detail as I can, which ends up reflecting quite a bit about my personal tastes and interests. In that, I think there is a story.

Excerpt I: mm. 1–14

Performance Advice on Excerpt I

The first line of the piece is quite difficult. I suggest first considering and practicing the nature and texture of the roll, from the beginning to the downbeat of m. 5, and adding in the accented A-flat and B-flat interjections afterwards. Steve describes what he wants very well, but it does not correspond to any typical marimba technique! So, think of the opening in new terms; be most concerned with how it sounds and the effect it has, unrelated to any technique you have ever tried before.

Begin the opening roll with a clean ***pp*** entrance (all four notes together) and get into making the most beautiful roll possible through the *crescendo*; make it *glow*! Shortly after the downbeat of m. 2, you should gradually start to press too much so that it begins to sound a bit awkward and ugly and, at the same, begin to make the alternations of your strokes uneven. By m. 3 it should sound quite *unlike* a nice roll—almost like you've never held sticks before! I use a ripple roll from the beginning so that, by the time my roll starts to break down, the quasi-dead-stroke hits in each hand are flams (left over from the ripple roll). By m. 3 I try to make the hits really quite jerky, with quite a lot of space in between them, in order to make it clear that I am *trying* to sound bad for an effect. (If you don't go a little over the top with trying to "sound bad," people will not get the idea that this is what is *supposed* to happen!) By m. 4, I begin to concern myself with connecting to m. 5, at which point it should not be noticeable that you have begun to play written music. To make this connection happen, I try to make some of my jerkiness in m. 4 hint at the material in m. 5. Then you just *slip* into m. 5!

Of course, you have to get so you can play those accented A-flat and B-flat interjections *on top of* the roll textures I described from the opening through m. 4. The other tricky thing is that all of what I described above happens in very quick succession! In the first five measures you are showing that this piece is going to be beautiful, yet a little strange, and that smooth transformations between those worlds could be a focal point in themselves.

Try to show the difference between the phrased and unphrased material from m. 5 onward. To achieve this, think of the material within each phrase mark as having a very subtle hairpin *diminuendo* beneath it. The marking "mechanical" will be quite convincing then, if in contrast to the phrased material, it is without dynamic nuance. There is an overall *diminuendo* at that point, but I mainly try to dry up my tone there by playing more articulately, and trying to sound like I'm speaking in a monotone. Notice the unusual way many of the sixteenth notes are beamed; I think of this as a suggestion for extremely subtle phrasing (and might give very slight emphasis to the first note of each beamed group).

Remember that all staccato notes are to be played as dead strokes or quasi-dead strokes throughout the piece.

Excerpt II: pick-up to m. 108 through m. 157

Note: Stickings added here indicate what I use, but are only suggestions.

123
graceful
mf
mp
126
129
132
135
Rit. = 54
gradually decrease trem. speed
into speed of triplet quarters
mp
p
mf

*Slightly irregular rhythmically, except where noted, like "random raindrops."
The total length of each irregular bar should be as if it had been played evenly.

Performance Advice on Excerpt II

Do as much *crescendo* as you can on the split bar roll in mm. 108 and 109. Bring out the "graceful" quality beginning in m. 125 by accentuating the "waltzyness" of the triplets; I also try to create a florid elegance by articulating the sixteenth notes within the triplet groupings as much as possible. The succession of events in mm. 136–138 should be extremely smooth: the joining of the high F-sharp, the departure of the G after the slowing-down of the roll, which should lead seamlessly into the quarter-note triplets (rather than the triplet grouping being clearly discernible).

Starting at m. 139, the notes add up to a fairly static texture despite the subtly shifting harmonies. The focal point becomes the mood created by the irregular notes. We can easily recognize them as something we know from nature (for instance, raindrops on a metal roof), yet they occur so infrequently in written music that there is something slightly eerie about them. I also try to create interest with four different types of strokes/touch in this section: (1) normal, on notes with no articulations marked; (2) dead-strokes on the staccatos; (3) full and long on the bass notes (marked with tenutos and accents); and (4) extremely legato on the notes marked with just tenutos. I achieve the latter by almost keeping the mallet on the bar after the point of contact—a kind of dead-stroke-without-dampening.

Excerpt III: mm. 271–289

Performance Advice on Excerpt III

Despite the page-turn break and shift in texture here, this section is actually a continuation of the Thelonious Monk section. The "oom-pahs" (which began on the low A in m. 249) continually descend to their ultimate goal, the C-sharp in m. 299.

The challenge here is to articulate the octaves well, adhere to the dynamics, and play very rhythmically (except where there are fermatas). Just the act of being in firm control of those things goes a long way toward creating the feeling of "suppressed intensity." To me, the alternation of the fast, quirky octave runs with the oom-pah figures has enormous expressive possibilities. The octave figures seem to have a nervous, worried or pressured quality (one kind of "intensity"), while the oom-pah figures give the sense of calm, poise, maybe even wisdom (another, quieter kind of intensity). In effect, we're overhearing a conversation between these states of mind. Maybe they're a bit shy around each other, sensing how different the other is (hence, the "suppressed" quality)! I try to bring out the differences between them by articulating the octave passages as well as possible, and playing the oom-pahs as deeply and richly as possible.

The octave passages here present a fantastic example of material that could be developed into little exercises, which will both improve your technique and your ability to play this section of "See Ya Thursday." Here's an example of the kind of exercises I often invent to warm-up before performing this piece. Of course, you could repeat these sorts of patterns any number of times until you have increased your control of them.

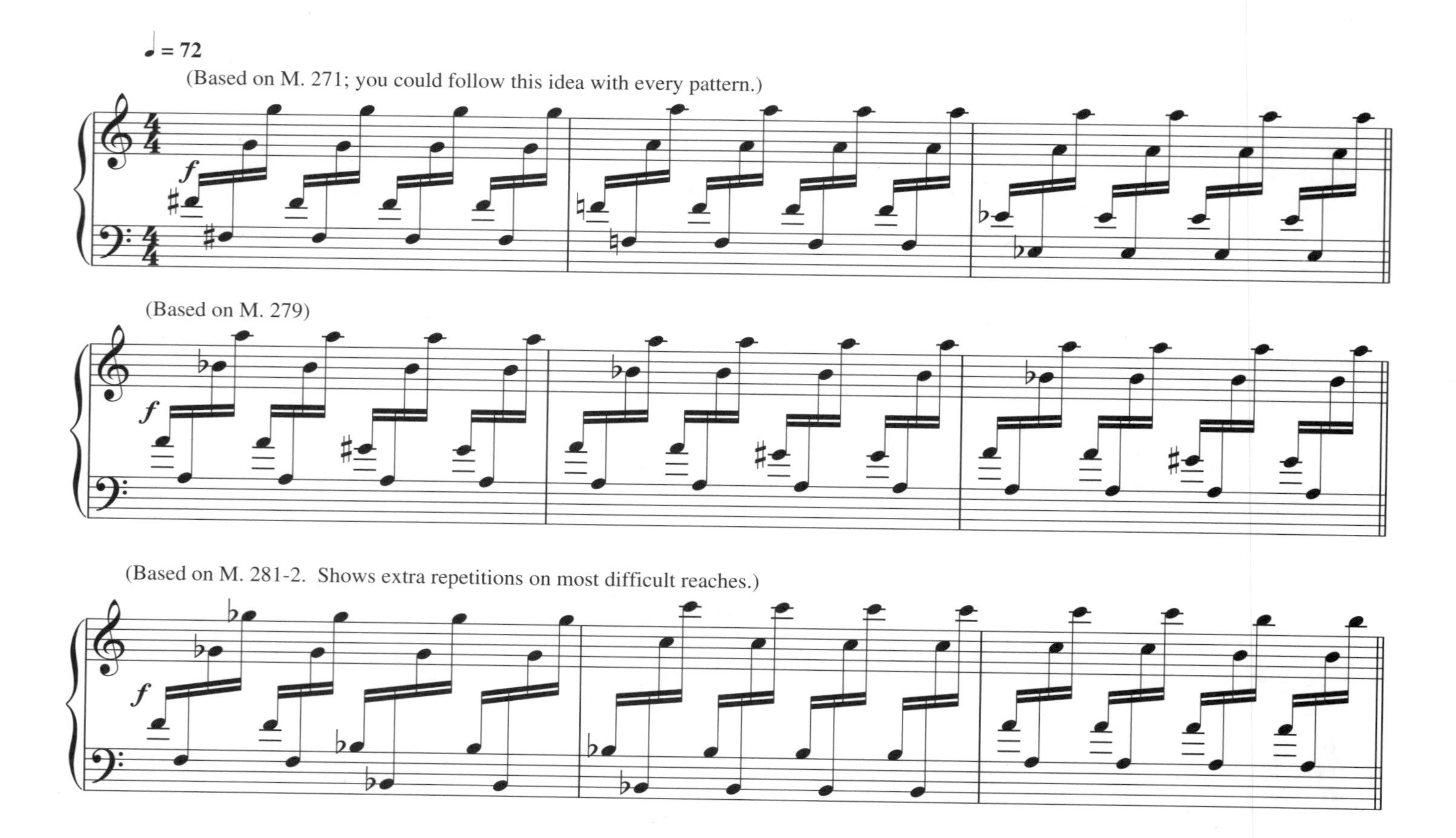

Excerpt IV: pick-up to m. 316 through m. 339 (downbeat)

Performance Advice on Excerpt IV

This is an interesting section, as it forces you to keep track of an unusual collection of things: big leaps, dead vs. normal strokes, small recurring phrases in both the right and left hands which are juxtaposed in different ways. Remember that, aside from the two-note right-hand phrases that are marked, you should imagine phrase marks between the bass and tenor notes (oom-pahs) in mm. 316–322. In mm. 323–326, there is an unusual series of these that are reversed (tenor-to-bass). The tenor note preceding the bass note briefly turns into a kind of pick-up-note in mm. 327–333, then things shift again and, in mm. 334–338, the first tenor note should be emphasized at the beginning of the phrase. Again, I accomplish this using dynamics. I put a little emphasis on the beginning of each phrase and imagine there's a subtle hairpin *diminuendo* under the subsequent notes within each phrase mark. (It's challenging to do this without dynamically affecting the notes in the right hand.)

Beginning in m. 312, I stick the three-note chords differently than Steve implies with his stems up/stems down notation. He implies that, for example, in m. 316 (although it begins in m. 312), the octave F-naturals are part of the same voice as the E, while the B-flat is another voice. Many people assume they should therefore play the octave in the right hand, and the single B-flat in the left. It's much simpler to play the top two notes in the right hand and the bottom note in the left. I think this is fine since the note durations *are* all eighths, and I can still bring out the phrasing of the notes in spite of my sticking. Also, when you get to m. 325, the right hand fifth is then the same as you had been playing all along.

Miscellaneous extra advice

- mm. 43–58 "sostenuto, in sweeping, 'spacey' waves": To me, this section is a chance (one of many in this piece) to play simple, exposed notes with the most beautiful, full tone possible. Again, slow downstrokes can help to achieve legato. "Sweeping, 'spacey'" suggests to me that the time can be very slightly toyed with in any manner that enhances the legato and brings as much meaning as possible to the note shifts in the right hand. Really enjoy how the marimba's beautiful natural decay has a chance to be heard here.
- mm. 61–63: It's fine to play the roll as a split-bar roll. However, if you decide to play it measured, my secret is to play the one-handed roll (with elbow turned inward; I step to the left so my arm can be extended most naturally) with mallet 3 in the middle beating spot and mallet 4 on the edge beating spot. I start it with the inner mallet, then I stick the last four sixteenths of the 5/8: (mallets) 2, 2, 3, 2.
- m. 207: The marking "playful, exuberant" should be a new feeling or attitude you're leading up to, as the harmony shifts and dynamic shapes evolve on page 6. It is a point of arrival, like when you realize "Hey! We're *here!*" at a place or situation you find exciting.
- m. 249–270: This section should be played in rather strict tempo. I like to practice this with a Dr. Beat metronome playing sixteenth-note subdivisions. It should groove! I play the roll in m. 264 as a one-handed roll (with my elbow turned in, so again I step a little to the left to facilitate this). It doesn't need to be very clear or perfect; it's a decoration within the context of a Thelonious Monkesque romp!
- m. 294–296: These measures pose problems for many players. I start the right-hand roll one-handed. Then, in m. 295, I very smoothly (hopefully!) change to a two-handed roll (in order to have optimum control of the *crescendo*); then, toward the end of m. 295, I switch back to a one-handed roll in the right hand.
- m. 343 and 345: I play all the rolls one-handed. They're difficult—especially the louder ones in the left hand; just do your best. (To be honest, if you keep good control of the one in the right hand, the one in the left hand isn't nearly as important as the accents.)
- m. 357: I strike the whole chord (at different dynamics in each hand, as indicated) and then use a two-handed roll on the high E and F.
- m. 358–363: This passage is really difficult! My goal in playing it is to absolutely know where bass notes (and ideal beating spots) are *by feel* (even though they're far away!).
- m. 376–end: Be careful not to play m. 376 too quickly. It's easy to do, because things have been so wild leading into it. There's a nice little melody hidden in there between the B-flat, D-flat, and A-flat. The piece, in a sense, ends in m. 390, and the rest is a little tag—like an afterthought.

"See Ya Thursday" was recorded by Nancy Zeltsman on the CD *See Ya Thursday* (Equilibrium EQ29).

Merlin (1985)
(in two movements)
for solo marimba

by Andrew Thomas (b. 1939)

Andrew Thomas
Photo by Howard L. Kessler

Errata/Notes (for movement II)

- m. 53, lower staff: Ossia for second sixteenth note is F-sharp 8va; ossia for seventh and eighth sixteenth notes is to play the D-sharp with the A rather than the F-sharp. (W.M.)*
- m. 71, upper staff: Ninth sixteenth-note double-stop should be B-natural and F.
- m. 145, lower staff: F should be F-sharp.
- m. 176, lower staff: In the manuscript, the first sixteenth note D (after the rest) also had a D 8ba (that is, an octave). The same was true for the last sixteenth note D in that bar. (W.M.)
- m. 177, lower staff: In the manuscript, the fifth sixteenth note had a middle C-sharp, not a sixteenth rest. (W.M.)

* Items marked "(W.M.)" were noted by William Moersch (who commissioned the work, and to whom it is dedicated) in *Percussive Notes*, Vol. 35, No. 5, October 1997, page 60.

General Advice

Thomas supplies two excerpts from a long poem called "Merlin" by Edwin Arlington Robinson—a narrative retelling of the King Arthur legend and the destruction of his court—to set the tone for each of the movements. My personal feeling is that it should be left up to each performer how much they wish to take that story into account as they play the piece. For me, the excerpts themselves conjure up a mood that I find useful to my personal imagery, and that is the extent to which I utilize the quotes by Robinson. For others, it might be fun to read the entire poem and learn more about the King Arthur legend for ideas to relate to the music. This raises the subject of imagery related to developing an interpretation of, or outlook on, a piece you will perform, which is addressed in Section III-G. How to Practice.

Performance Advice on Movement I

In approaching this movement, it's important to keep in mind the depth of inspiration behind it. Andrew Thomas described, "The chord sequences in the first movement came to me in about fifteen minutes, after which, I found to my surprise, that I had become tearful. It then took several weeks to make the chord sequences 'breathe.' This was surprisingly hard work, and I spent a lot of time walking around my studio, sensing the phrase lengths on my body, and then, trying to transfer them so that they spoke on the marimba in a way that was natural to the marimba's personality." Thomas succeeded beautifully in notating a sense of grandeur and depth. Playing this movement thoughtfully should leave you absolutely winded, and rather emotionally drained.

An important feature of the first movement is its two tempi. The opening (slower) tempo of "quarter = 40–50 ca." applies to mm. 1–12, 21–24, 32 (plus pick-up)–end. The "slightly faster" tempo (which I take at about quarter = 60) applies to mm. 13–20 and mm. 25–31 (or, actually, about m. 29). To mentally (and physically) ingrain the difference between these tempi, I suggest that you put on a metronome at quarter note = 46 (for the slower tempo) and try walking around a room, taking concentrated steps, imagining this as the pace of a dignified procession. It's a bit difficult to keep your balance at this tempo. Then, turn up the metronome to quarter note = 60 and walk around for awhile. Notice that it is quite a bit easier to keep your balance; in fact it's about the slowest tempo at which it's still relatively easy to keep your balance. I think contemplating these two tempi in this way is very helpful in memorizing them and keeping steady.

There is some ambiguity in the score as to exactly when the tempi change, but I tend to trust the spatial notation of where the changes are indicated. I try to think of the faster tempo beginning on beat two of m. 13, and the slower tempo beginning on beat 2 of m. 21. I think the slow tempo returns in m. 31 on beat 4. At these points, I literally begin to breathe differently, as if I can mandate a shift in my body metabolism, right at that moment, to the different (slower or faster) mode of being.

People are often confused by Thomas' note at the beginning, "Play all tremolos as independent rolls." He was using the word "independent" in its most literal meaning; he wants rolls in which the mallets strike independently of one another. Technically, this is most often called a ripple roll. He does *not* want two one-handed rolls (as are sometimes called "independent" rolls).

I usually use quite soft mallets for this movement: a combination such as Encore NZ8,5,5,4. As with all rolls on chords that begin a phrase (even at soft dynamics), I suggest entering the first four-note chord with all four mallets striking together. Then concentrate on all voices being heard equally.

Throughout the movement (as well as most all chorales), always be aware in which voice(s) note(s) are about to change, and lean on them a little. For instance, by the third beat of m. 1, slightly accentuate the D in the tenor mallet, in order to highlight the beat 4 change to C-sharp in that voice. Then balance all the voices again, but slightly emphasize the top three notes in the *crescendo*, as all three are about to change pitch (etc.).

Make sure the grace-note figures are not too soft. They are an important, recurring feature in the movement and must have a certain amount of presence in order to be recognizable as such. I like to play the flam quite open, to help the figure be more recognizable. Another reason it is important for the figure to be clearly audible is that "on the beat" means that the grace note is played on the beat (rather than the note immediately following it). The relative placement of beat 2 is, therefore, very important, as the precise distance between the grace note and beat 2 establishes the tempo.

On the other side of the dynamic spectrum, I recommend downplaying all the louder dynamics on the first page so that you can keep the dynamic tiers properly related to the peak of the movement in m. 27. For instance, if you play the ***mf*** in m. 7 too loudly, it will be impossible to surpass it with the ***f*** in mm. 11, 13, and 16, and surpass it again with the ***ff*** in m. 25, and then again with the peak ***fff*** in m. 27—all in equal increments! So, I try to think of the ***mf***s and ***f***s on page one as having a minus sign after them. Try to make the sound very full and rich, yet not that loud.

Remember to breathe between phrases, and especially at the breath marks. For instance, in m. 6, finish one phrase, and let there be a tiny feeling of lift or air (that is, a small space) before the next phrase settles in. When there are breath marks, literally *inhale*! When the following entrance is soft, as in mm. 11 and 37, it will help you to enter in a more hushed fashion. When the following entrance is loud, as in mm. 25, 36 and 42, it will help you to feel the majesty of the loud music that is about to enter, as well as add suspense for your audience regarding *when* the "bomb" is going to drop!

An interesting feature of this movement is that much of the forward motion takes place on off-beats (relative to the main beats of the measures). Therefore, I think it's important to count the music as it is written and notice what falls on off-beats and what falls on main beats. One particular spot in which a lot of players fail to do this is between mm. 16–20. For some reason, coming off the "mini-3/8 bar" (at the beginning of m. 16), a surprising number of people just count two beats per chord until the final one in the phrase. But, I find much more meaning in this phrase if you recognize every change is on an off-beat. (By the way, don't forget that the flat on the B in m. 19 holds through the bar.)

Excerpt I: Movement I, mm. 25–31

Performance Advice on Excerpt I

The excerpt above is probably the most difficult section of the first movement insofar as it demands excellent mallet control during rolls on wide intervals (mostly octaves) over fairly long durations at a loud dynamic. There are some tricks you can do to make it easier, which also flatter the music. First, give a clean attack—all four notes striking simultaneously—on every accented chord (even the ***p*** one). This differentiates the accented chords from the unaccented ones, and also helps boost the dynamic. To play the ***fff***, refer to my guidelines on "Playing Loudly" in Section III-A. Refining Strokes and Tone Production. It adds excitement to increase your roll speed there, too. Take advantage of the "*accel. pochiss.*" and push the tempo through this difficult section. You will be more likely to "give your all" if it isn't too stretched out. Then, you can enhance the "*rit. pochiss.*" and "*dim.*" by also gradually relaxing your roll speed. I would keep the roll at a steady, though relaxed, speed by the time you reach the final ***p*** chord.

Performance Advice on Movement II

The biggest mistake people make with this movement is trying to play it too fast. Thomas' intention in marking "dotted quarter = 72 ca." was to give an *approximate* tempo, not invite a race! What he cares about most is that the movement dances and grooves. Proof of that is the intricate articulations and phrasing nuances he wrote, which are inspired and inspiring! If you blow past them, they're pointless. There are the accents versus tenutos, various playful patterns of two- and three-note groupings, and many different and suggestive note-beamings. Thomas also doesn't intend for the tempo to remain robotically even throughout. He is not at all opposed to some rubato, if the performer utilizes it convincingly to enhance the tension in the work.

My favorite mallets for this movement are a slightly worn out Encore "NZ Graduated Set of 4" (which consists of NZ6,4,3,2). Many people use harder mallets, but I feel they accentuate the attack of the notes too much. My selection tends to emphasize the fundamentals, which in turn makes the harmonies richer. An excellent example is mm. 25–29. With an NZ6 mallet in the bass, I can really dig into the bass accents. In order to play those accents appropriately with harder mallets (to avoid cracking them!), I couldn't "dig in" as much, which would forfeit some musical excitement.

Excerpt II: Movement II, mm. 1–14

Performance Advice on Excerpt II

An interesting feature of the first line of music is that the two- and three-note grouping patterns—for the first two measures from left to right, and for mm. 3 and 4 from right to left—match! I think of the opening two lines as the introduction of the accents, and the next four lines—which, being rumbly and rhythmic (especially in mm. 9–14), I have nick-named "the tom-tom section"—as the introduction of the tenutos (as well as interplay between tenutos and accents). To review how I try to differentiate between accents and tenutos: I bring out the accents with a quick, snappy stroke (taking care to compensate for how fast the stroke arrives, so that I am placing notes accurately); and I use a languid, heavy (from-the-shoulder) stroke on the tenutos.

In the opening crescendo, take care that *both* hands crescendo, not just the right hand. The fourth sixteenth note of m. 5 is an important, explosive arrival point. For me, it helps to imagine that, beginning there, the rest of m. 5 and m. 6 is actually written in the following meters: 4/8, 4/16, 3/16, 3/8. For fun, note that, like the opening line, the rhythmic groupings in m. 7, from left to right, are just like the ones in m. 8, from right to left!

Beginning in m. 10 there is a journey through distinct dynamic plateaus. Try to maintain a fairly consistent ***p*** throughout mm. 10–13; then make a subtle, controlled *crescendo* up to ***mp***. (Continue to make each dynamic plateau clear through m. 24.)

Some patterns of two- and three-note groupings occur more frequently within the movement than others. For instance, at m. 37, the combination of 3+2+3+2+2 remains constant through m. 42. (I tend to think of mm. 31–33 as its introduction.) That pattern returns in mm. 141–147, 151 and 152, and 154–168. Another common one is 2+3+2+3+2, which is introduced in mm. 34 and 35, and then established in mm. 57–68. It recurs in mm. 70–89 (perhaps the most important development section), 92 and 93, 104 and 105, 109–112, 170–180 (which includes the climax of the movement, mm. 176–179), and 208–end.

Notice that those patterns are really the same, except that the second one begins with the final "2" of the first one. Thomas also uses other permutations of the pattern. Its playfulness stems from the constant alternation of the two- and three-note groups—except for the shift of placement of the two consecutive "twos." I think the important thing is that, when one pattern settles in for a while, it really "grooves." (Imagine there is suddenly a hand-drummer laying down that pattern with you!) Thomas says that the places in which a rhythmic pattern repeats for several measures are "moments of relative balance and repose in the music."

Another playful thing Thomas layered on top of all that is a varied approach to beaming. Sometimes, as in m. 37, each group is beamed separately. Oftentimes, there is a combined set of groups followed by two short ones, as in m. 70. Other times, the combined set of groups comes in the middle of the bar, as in m. 106. I try to interpret these is as if they are mini-phrases. I try to play slightly more legato across the combined groups, with a tiny separation between the short groups. This is not easy! But when you do succeed, it really "percolates"!

Excerpt III: Movement II, mm. 52–56

Performance Advice on Excerpt III (and Beyond)

The stickings I use in this difficult spot are offered here as a suggestion. (They break all my basic "rules"!) You may wish to instead use slightly different stickings and/or try the "ossias" offered in the Errata section at the beginning of this chapter. It doesn't hurt to begin this passage a little slowly, if it helps you get your bearings. In very difficult passages such as this, it's a strange but natural tendency to rush. If we can remember to do the opposite, it will help us to think more clearly and help the listener hear the intricacies of the passage. This is certainly true of this section, which is in a murky register of the marimba.

One trick for playing the octave passages at the end (and similar passages later in the piece) is, for those who have one hand that is weaker than the other (in my case, the left), imagine you are leading with the *weaker* hand, which will help to push that hand.

In the two "Calypso sections" (again, my nickname), mm. 37–51 and 57–66, consider the balance between your hands, as well as how the sections relate to each other. The melody in the right hand, which highlights the two- and three-note groupings, is infectious and groovy and many people are drawn to bringing it out. However, I suggest not doing so; because it is the top voice, it will quite easily be heard. Instead, I would try to draw attention to the three-note phrases marked with tenutos in the left hand: bass, tenor, and alto pitches. Take care to bring out the alto note of each phrase. (Because it enters the register of the right-hand melody, it can get swallowed up; you want to make it clear that it is part of the left-hand phrases.) One fun thing to practice is singing the three-note tenuto phrases while you play!

The same applies to the balance between hands in mm. 57–66, but here there is the added issue of the phrase markings. My trick (as with executing most phrases) is imagining subtle hairpin *diminuendos* from the first to the last note of each phrase. This section (while still being soft), should have a lovely, lively "sway" to it. In contrast, the first "Calypso" section is a bit more reserved and upright in feeling.

At m. 68, despite the beaming on the bottom staff, I would suggest sticking the three lowest notes with mallets 1, 2, and 3. Playing the C-sharp and G with the right hand (given the inward wrist turn necessary to play the C-sharp) makes the jump to the top-staff notes much too difficult.

Excerpt IV: Movement II, mm. 70–93

Performance Advice on Excerpt IV

Thomas intends for idea of the left-hand's three-note tenuto phrases (notated in the "Calypso" sections) to continue through the entire next section, mm. 70–89, even though they are not marked.

It was a revelation to me when Mr. Thomas sat down at the piano once and played for me the composite chords that can be derived from the passages indicated in Excerpt IV between the markings "/" and "\" (for beginnings and endings). I have also written them as clusters below. They make clear how critical note accuracy is in this section (so that you not destroy these beautiful harmonies). Also, hearing the clusters inspired me to adjust my touch through this section to play more warmly in order to bring out the composite "clouds of sound," as opposed to being extremely articulate.

M.73 M.75 (w/pick-up) M.76 (w/pick-up) M.77 & 78 M.78 & 79 M.80 (w/pick-up)

M.81 (w/pick-up) M.82 (M.83) M.85 & 86 M.87 & 88 M.89 M.92 & 93

Performance Advice on mm. 90–120

Don't hesitate to use rubato getting into the octave runs beginning in m. 90 and m. 94. It helps make them more dramatic (and it helps make them more playable!).

In playing the double tritones beginning in the second half of m. 96, you should match the tempo at which you played the end of the octave run (which should be about dotted quarter = 72); many people make the mistake of suddenly playing faster. Also, slightly emphasize the first chord of each three-grouping in order to clarify how they are notated. (Otherwise, the first chord can be mistaken for a pick-up into the second chord.)

Be careful not to overplay the *sfz* in m. 99, and especially the ***f***s in m. 101 (as well as the big chords later in mm. 119 and 120). The tone quality of these will be much nicer if you don't "slam" them. Your sound will be warmer if you prepare to play the chords before you do so, rather than playing them "on the fly."

Excerpt V: Movement II, mm. 113–118

Performance Advice on Excerpt V

This section is included to offer my stickings as one possibility. These *do* follow most of my sticking rules (except for a few triple stickings, and not playing some important notes with a "clean hand"). They are a good example of how to choose stickings for notes spanning many octaves so that you can end up using as little movement as possible. Note that I avoided using mallet 1 except on the lowest notes since, with graduated mallets, it might produce too soft a tone in the middle and high registers. I recommend at some point practicing playing *only* the accents, so that you learn where *not* to play them (m. 114, beat 1, and last three-grouping of m. 115).

It is (perhaps) obvious that the roll-interjections in mm. 132, 136 and 137, and 140 hearken back to the first movement. I tend to languish in these a little. Don't stray too far from the main tempo, but if the tempo relaxes a bit, it will help remind listeners of the mood of the first movement.

Excerpt VI: Movement II, mm. 189–200

Performance Advice for Excerpt VI

This is an excellent section for practicing playing with a big, full tone. To achieve this, I recommend using somewhat slow, heavy strokes rather than snappy, articulate ones. It's also a great etude for maintaining interval sizes (fourths and fifths) while making small leaps.

Many people wonder why the last two sixteenth notes in m. 196 are written in parentheses. It's because it is optional to play them (but most people do).

I recommend practicing the thirty-second-note runs in mm. 201–205 slowly, accentuating the note groupings (sixes and fours). Also, I like to use my 1 and 3 mallets for the lower notes and, at some point, switch to my 2 and 4 mallets for the highest notes, etc. If you can't reach the spread written at the end of m. 205, play the left hand 8va until the seventh sixteenth note in m. 206, then return to what's written. For the finale, mm. 208–end, I recommend bringing out the two- and three-note groupings, as well as emphasizing the first beat of every bar, so it is fairly clear that you end on an upbeat.

One final word (which applies to the entire piece): I have heard Andrew Thomas discuss his concerns about performers overplaying loud dynamics on the marimba. "Merlin" inspires very excited playing and provides the opportunity to make wonderful dynamic contrasts. but keep in mind that Thomas has written this piece (and so many other wonderful pieces) for the marimba because he deeply loves the tone and natural character of the instrument. He greatly appreciates hearing his music played with respect given to those features.

"Merlin" was recorded by Nancy Zeltsman on the CD *Woodcuts* (GM Recordings GM2043CD).

WORKS FOR VIOLIN AND MARIMBA

Robert Aldridge with Nancy Zeltsman

threedance (1987)
for violin, marimba and tabla/triangle

by Robert Aldridge (b. 1954)

(Note: the violin and tabla play throughout most of these excerpts, even though only the marimba part is provided here.)

Excerpt I: mm. 1–18

Performance Advice on Excerpt I

For mallets, I would use an NZ5 in the bass, a slightly worn-out NZ3 for mallet 2, and slightly worn-out NZ2s in the right hand. Your playing should be extremely incisive and articulate at the beginning, and throughout most of the piece, and these mallets will help. However, they also have enough body that you will be able to get a warm sound in certain sections.

Try to remain articulate through mm. 6 and 7, which are a bit challenging. The stickings included show my preference to use some double-stickings here, as I can get more volume and intensity with them, rather than continuing the ripple stickings. (Practicing the Double-Sticking Exercise in Section III-B. Relationship of Sticking Choices to Phrasing will help.) Notice that there's a rare moment at the end of m. 9 in which I would keep the ripple pattern going and play the last two sixteenth notes with two rights (mallets 4 and 3) even though they lead into a very important, sharp downbeat in m. 10 played again with the right hand. Do your best to throw your mallets out to reach the interval of a ninth.

There are a lot of ninths (and other large intervals) in "threedance." They can be especially challenging in the left hand (because of the wider bar widths in the lower register). I play these with my hand as far back as possible on the mallet handles. (The end of mallet 1 is almost flush with the side of my left hand.) I hold the mallets with only my 5th finger (the 4th finger is quite far away from the mallets on intervals this big). Remember how your hand feels in this position. You will need to "throw out" the mallets into ninth intervals frequently throughout the piece, so you want your hand to "memorize" the feel of that position, which will "catch" them.

Bear in mind that the stick clicks in m. 1 are part of the piece. Don't hesitate to be a little theatrical; raise your sticks near your face and *go to it!* Your body language should invite your partners to attack m. 2 with you, and set the tone that the piece will indeed be "fast and furious."

At letter A you must immediately shift gears and not only play softer, but with a much fuller tone. This is an awkward spot; after the bombastic and busy introduction, it feels strange to play "a touch slower" here as well as so much simpler. Focusing on the difficult task of playing with a rich sound here—with slow, caressing strokes—can help make this transition. Instead of losing intensity, think in terms of channeling the intensity differently.

Excerpt II: mm. 115–141

Performance Advice on Excerpt II

There are incessant meter changes in this piece, but this section is one of the most challenging in this regard. I try to always be reading ahead to see what meter is coming, in order to know whether I will be thinking in groupings of two or three. All the while, I am maniacally subdividing eighth notes. It helps to give a little emphasis on every downbeat (where you can) to keep the meters clear and to stay synchronized with the other players—the tabla in particular.

Besides the meter issues, the dynamics in this section are wild. There are the rapid swoops between ***p*** and ***f*** at the beginning and, later, the dynamic dips down to ***p*** in between brief *subito* ***f*** and ***ff*** (and, in m. 149, ***fff***) plateaus. The right hand should be very prominent in the latter loud sections. You can almost disappear in the ***p***'s. In contrast to all that schizophrenic activity, be careful to keep the *crescendo* in mm. 126–132 very gradual.

Here you are tested further on throwing out to the wide ninth intervals I mentioned earlier. If you just can't get the hang of it, it might be wise to have some special mallets made with handles that are an inch longer.

Excerpt III: mm. 191–198

Performance Advice on Excerpt III

Robert Aldridge has an uncanny knack for writing idiomatic hand-to-hand marimba music that is fun to play. But, inherent in how comfortably it lies in your hands is the danger that you will rush the tempo. The trick is to always keep track of the subdivisions. (You could loop the passage above to create a fun exercise.)

Excerpt IV: mm. 219–229

Performance Advice on Excerpt IV

This excerpt is like Excerpt III in that one must be careful not to close up the figures and rush. Mallets 4 and 3 seem to fall into an easy rolling motion, but you can, at the same time, be carefully placing each sixteenth note. Try to also bring out the phrase groupings (by leaning a little on the first notes of each), as well as the way they overlap each other between hands. In mm. 225–228, notice that I would do double stickings. These are by no means easy, but I think it's easier to control the dynamic this way. (If you were to try to continue the 4 to 3 sticking, there would be a tendency, especially coming off the G-sharp/D-sharp, to accent the E with mallet 4 because it requires an awkward lunge.)

Excerpt V: mm. 266–281

Performance Advice on Excerpt V

The first five bars of this excerpt are a solo. The challenge here is to make the sound quality as lush as possible. With the lowest note being A, there is the danger that the piece as a whole can seem to lack sufficient bass. Here, especially, make the low A as rich as you can. When the tabla joins you on the downbeat of m. 270, it should get the deepest pitch possible before scooping up.

Excerpt VI: mm. 482–497

Performance Advice in Except VI

This is a challenging passage because note accuracy is so critical; for much of it, you are playing in unison with the violin. My partner and I practiced this slowly many times to ensure that we had digested the subtle inner-note changes, which are critical to the harmonic movement.

This is a fantastic section for developing your ability to find the notes by feel. I suggest keeping mallets 1 and 2 in place (on the low A and gradually changing tenor notes) so that you can concentrate on each upcoming group of inner notes and high accented note. Learn where the notes are by feel and trust yourself!

When you need to play notes that encompass a wide registral span like this, concentrate on your center of gravity. (I often tense my stomach muscles in much the same way as when I'm trying to keep my torso erect while picking up a heavy box using my legs. Reading the music that is directly in front of me serves to positively reinforce my feeling of being centered.) This is one spot in which playing many consecutive rights (altering only how mallets 3 and 4 negotiate the inner notes to minimize movement, given the various wrist twists involved) is safest and sounds best.

General Advice

This piece has an absolutely thrilling energy, largely due to its breakneck pace. It's also extremely passionate and sensual. Ultimately it requires you to meet intense technical demands, maintain extreme concentration and, at the same time, give your all emotionally. Consider some of the performance directives given: "always exaggerated dynamics," "vibrant and joyous," "always sweet and delicate," "gradually agitated, as in a bad dream," "gradually calm," "increasingly wild," "very expansively, with liquid legato," "molto agitato," "with abandon," "molto agitato, exploding with passion," "with total abandon."

The list itself gives a sense of the emotional undulations in the piece. In some sections, your ensemble can enhance this by being somewhat elastic with the tempo. One spot is the section beginning at letter B: mm. 79 (until around m. 106). While musicians generally need to resist the tendency to push the tempo when making a *crescendo* and relax the tempo while making a *diminuendo*, in this section it works beautifully if you give in and do this! It may work best if the marimba player leads it.

Another section in which the tempo can be a bit flexible is mm. 266–299 (and, to some degree, continuing through m. 326). Here, I wouldn't push ahead or pull back following dynamics so much. Instead, I would be a bit flexible *within* each measure by sinking into each downbeat (that is, trying to get an especially rich tone, and putting some extra space around them) and giving each accented right-hand note a bit of extra time to ring. Also, really let the measures of rest *breathe* (if anything, stretch the time a bit; don't cheat it). It is up to you to create a sensual mood, which becomes a backdrop/support for the violinist.

The marimba and tabla are meant to play together throughout most of the piece as one "super-percussion" instrument. As I said before, you must do your best to be convincing that the piece has enough "bottom." (To reiterate, it is critical that your bass mallet is not too hard or the fundamental of the low A will not be audible.) The tabla player should also be sensitive to the need to emphasize low pitches. The violin part plays extremely high in spots. Considering that, you want to create the largest pitch spectrum possible.

I know it can be difficult to find a great tabla player. I have also heard the tabla part played on dumbek, and it was a fine substitution (although tabla add a bit more depth).

Finally, regarding the logistics of page turns, this is one piece in which I do not hesitate to throw the music on the floor. Many people feel that pages of music should never be thrown on the floor (it could appear disrespectful to the music). In this case, the marimba part is laid out in three big sections of multiple pages. Personally, I don't think there is sufficient time between sections to do something "polite" with the music. I think it's most important to get the old pages out of the way as quickly and quietly as possible, in order to keep your focus on the next entrance. Given the "wild and wooly" nature of this piece, I don't feel this detracts from the music or appears disrespectful in the least. To me, it is a necessity that could even be seen as being in spirit of the piece, and will be completely understood.

"threedance" was recorded by Marimolin on the CD *Marimolin* (GM Recordings GM2023CD).

Gunther Schuller with Nancy Zeltsman
Photo by Allen Navratil

Phantasmata (1989)
for violin and marimba

by Gunther Schuller (b. 1925)

Excerpt I: Movement II, mm. 1–9 (marimba and violin)

Performance Advice on Excerpt I

In the first measure, both performers must clarify the pulse; the music should sound like it's in 4/4, not 3/8. To achieve this, the performers should play tiny accents on beats 2, 3, and 4. Play the ***sf***'s in m. 3 strongly, but keep a full tone. If the attacks are too sharp, the pitches will not be clear. m. 5 is one of the most difficult, rapidly shifting chordal passages I have had to play. (But conquering this one helped me immensely with all the similar passages I've come across since!) In m. 7, be sure to divide the triplets evenly; let them have an elegant, dance-like quality, which will be helped by tiny accents on beats 2 and 4. m. 8 is a big spread in the left hand, but you can utilize the preceding eighth-note rest to prepare for it.

Excerpt II: Movement IV, mm. 1–28 (marimba solo)

*Play staccatos as dead strokes.

a tempo
rit.
poco libero
sim.
switch upper 3 mallets to medium hard – quickly!

Performance Advice on Excerpt II

For this extensive marimba solo, Schuller liked me to use a huge, booming bass mallet. My mallets for this solo would probably be Encore Mallets NZ8,6,5,4. Then I'd quickly switch to harder mallets after m. 28 in the top three positions for the remainder of the movement. I have indicated a lot of stickings to show you interesting ways you can use the "boomer mallet" (8) to enhance sustain and/or low fundamentals. In m. 7, however, note that I do not recommend using the boomer mallet on the lowest pitches as it will muddle the number of notes in each group—which should be clear. By contrast, it is advantageous to use it for the bass notes in mm. 9 and 10, as these figures outline chords for which we want a fundamental-rich bass note. The same is true in mm. 25 and 26. We can even get away with using it for the same reason in m. 23 on the third beat (even though it resembles the figure beginning on the third beat in m. 7) because this figure's main function is more chordal than rhythmic.

Of course, it's rare to use such an extreme mallet as the "boomer bass mallet," but this is one case where the advantages (sustain, fundamental) outweigh the disadvantages. Besides being awkwardly heavy, it is difficult to roll between the boomer mallet and another mallet, as in the one-handed rolls in mm. 17–21. But try to first emphasize the strike with the boomer and then sneak into rolling, being extra light with the other mallet so that its attack (vs. the boomer's "non-attack") is minimized. Another problem is that the boomer mallet is completely inappropriate for use in the middle range of the instrument, which cannot be avoided at the end of the solo. Just do the best you can to get a clear attack with it. (Schuller definitely felt this compromise was worth having the boomer mallet for the rest of the solo.)

In mm. 25–27 you will see an unusual sticking notation, "4/SB." This means to attack the note with mallet 4, then jump to doing a split-bar roll. (Then, jump back to the normal playing position, as late as possible, to play the following grace-note figure.)

General Advice

This piece is full of big, thick, complicated chords. It is essential that both players hear them not as a big violin chord and a big marimba chord, but as huge, homogenized units, blended together as much as possible despite the obvious timbral differences between the instruments. To achieve this, I recommend playing through the score at a piano where it is easier to hear the composite chords. Play them repeatedly until you really hear and digest the accumulation of colors in them.

Schuller was adamant in our coachings that the marimba mallets should not be too hard. It's crucial to get as much fundamental pitch as possible (or none of the aforementioned chord balancing between the instruments will be discernible). Schuller feels very strongly that, for all his music, mallets should always be chosen for their ability to emphasize the fundamentals. Clarity of attack is always a secondary consideration for him.

"Phantasmata" was recorded by Marimolin on the CD *Phantasmata* (GM Recordings GM2048CD).

Alejandro Viñao
Photo by Kicca Tommasi

Tumblers (1990)
for violin, marimba and computer

by Alejandro Viñao (b. 1951)

Excerpt I: mm. 1–15 (marimba and computer only)

Performance Advice on Excerpt I

The opening encapsulates the rhythmic challenges of the piece. Throughout this work, the rhythms should *not* just swing somewhere between a duple and triple feel; they are meant to be played with extreme precision. A player needs to be able to "solfege" duple and triple rhythms as a backdrop to playing this music in order to be absolutely accurate. This is a prime time to utilize the tonguing technique suggested in Section I–G. Basics of Good Rhythm and "Feel." For mm. 2 and 3, for example, you would tongue to yourself (as you play):

Excerpt II: mm. 175–205 (predominantly marimba and computer; violin plays interjections)

185
sim.
190

Performance Advice on Excerpt II

The previous challenging excerpt provides an excellent technical study of hand-to-hand trade-offs. My choice of changing hands on the duple beats (beat "two-and") was somewhat arbitrary, but I purposely remained consistent with it. I chose to alternate hands, even on the sixteenth-note pick-ups (as opposed to playing them in one mallet), as I think it gives more lilt to the rhythms.

Be extremely accurate with the dynamics. The computer represents not only a driving, relentless force in the piece with regard to rhythms, but also in regard to dynamics. Viñao has prescribed them carefully to achieve the effect of two performers seeming in constant motion—alternately jutting-out and receding, or intertwining with each other and the computer—like tumblers.

Excerpt III: mm. 357–368 (marimba and computer)

Performance Advice on Excerpt III

This is an interesting spot in which to work on projecting accent vs. tenuto articulations. It can help to use a graduated set of mallets—perhaps (from left to right) Encore NZ5,3,2,2—and follow the sticking indicated. The result in mm. 360–365 is that the accents would all be played by harder mallets (NZ2s), and the tenutos would be played by a slightly softer mallet (an NZ3). In m. 368 the sticking indicated keeps all the tenutos in mallet 4 (or mallet 3) so that you can concentrate on maintaining a uniform, full-sounding stroke in one mallet.

Background Tidbit

Viñao had an interesting plan for introducing the piece to us. Once he completed it, and almost a month before he sent any written music, he sent two computer mock-up tapes of the entire piece (one for each performer: MIDI versions of the violin and marimba, plus computer). He asked us to immerse ourselves in it: to listen to it many times in many ways, from intent listening to having it on as background music. He wanted us to get accustomed to the rhythms and meter changes so that they felt familiar and natural—almost like pop music. It paid off; by the time we saw the score, we already knew how the phrases were supposed to flow and were therefore less intimidated by the notation.

General Advice

With regard to your general approach to tone/timbre when playing this piece (and the same goes for the violinist), see if you can mimic the electronic quality of the computer part. In general, this might mean going for sharper, biting attacks than you do ordinarily.

"Tumblers" demands enormous energy from the performers in order for it to be rendered with extreme precision: rhythmically, dynamically, timbrally, and musically. As the title implies, the piece should have an air of being an athletic feat; your performance should have a sense of muscularity about it. The tension inherent in meeting its challenges is exactly what makes the piece so clever, direct, and effective.

Viñao sent us those computer mock-up tapes as we were preparing to premiere the work, since no other recordings existed at the time. However, in May of 1991, Marimolin recorded "Tumblers" in London with Viñao present to approve the miking and produce the recording. He is very happy with the sound of that recording and says it "is what [he] had in mind all along." That recording and the performance materials for "Tumblers" are available from the composer at www.vinao.com.

About the Author

Nancy Zeltsman (b. 1958, Morristown, NJ) is a leading marimba performer, recording artist, commissioner of new works, teacher, and author. She has recorded two solo CDs, *Woodcuts* (GM Recordings) and *See Ya Thursday* (Equilibrium); and three CDs with the marimba/violin duo Marimolin: *Marimolin, Phantasmata* (GM Recordings) and *Combo Platter* (Catalyst/BMG, out of print). During its eleven years (1985–1996) Marimolin premiered nearly 80 pieces, sponsored eight annual international composition contests, and performed across the U.S. and in Europe. Numerous marimba solos and duos have also been composed for Nancy.

Zeltsman has taught marimba at the Boston Conservatory and Berklee College of Music since 1993. She is Artistic Director of The Zeltsman Marimba Festival, Inc. Zeltsman served on the jury of the 2001 Belgium International Marimba Competition and, in 1998, was one of twelve international players featured at the World Marimba Festival in Osaka, Japan. She has also presented numerous marimba master classes across the U.S. as well as in Europe, Japan, and Mexico.

Nancy is a graduate of New England Conservatory where she was a student of Vic Firth. Prior to that, she studied intensively with xylophonist Ian Finkel. Zeltsman endorses Marimba One marimbas and the Nancy Zeltsman Series of Encore Mallets. Visit her Web site at: www.nancyzeltsman.com